Start Something

Mathu Ardis Thomason

Scripture quotations are taken from the Holy Bible, New Living Translation, copyright ©1996, 2004, 2007, 2013, 2015 by Tyndale House Foundation. Used by permission of Tyndale House Publishers, Inc., Carol Stream, Illinois 60188. All rights reserved.

Cover Art by Margo Williams, Instagram: @howmargoseesart

Cover Design by Kevin John, Instagram: @kjd_sign
Website: www.simpleelms.com

ISBN 978-0998617206

Dedicated to

Aimee, Kindle and True.

I couldn't have done it without you.

And

To anyone who ever told me,

"You should write a book."

Thank you

Mom and Dad.

The depth of your love

And support still baffles me.

And

Debby,

For being the type of person

That travels to the other side of the world

To help a friend.

In memory of

Grandma 'Jeanie' Thomason.

You ran a good race, Grandma.

Contents

Foreword

Have you ever felt scared of something? I've felt afraid for most of my life – afraid of the dark, afraid of people's opinions, afraid of pain, afraid of broken relationships. Anytime I've wanted to do anything, immediately I can list a million reasons not to do that thing. But mostly, I'm just scared.

Several years ago, I spent the Fourth of July at Mat and Aimee Thomason's old apartment in Idaho. They had a get together with random friends and family, a pretty normal occurrence since love seemed to give their home elastic walls. At ten o'clock, we all climbed on top of a big garage, where we watched the fireworks exploding all around the suburbs.

Mat and Aimee have a daughter named Kindle. At the time she was pretty young, maybe three years old. Kindle was on the roof with us, tucked next to her mom. Once the fireworks had ended, we all made our way back down the roof of the garage. It was steep in places, so we were all stepping carefully in the dark.

Kindle became scared as she walked, and Aimee felt anxious about her little girl walking on the roof. Aimee asked Mat to carry Kindle, and Kindle started crying. "I can't," she cried, afraid of how steep the roof seemed.

Mat simply held Kindle's hand. "You can do it," he said. Aimee wasn't as sure; Kindle was still pretty small. "She can do it," Mat said. Kindle was scared, but Mat just kept saying, "You can do it." He held her hand firmly in his. There was no way she was going to fall. "You can do it." Again and again, he whispered courage into Kindle. She walked all the way off the roof, her little hand in Mat's the whole time. When she got to the end, Kindle's whole demeanor changed. "I did it!"

That memory has been engraved in my mind for years. It's given me some amazing insight into God's heart. I'm little Kindle. I'm scared. I can't move forward. I can't find my way out of this dark situation. "You can do it," God whispers. He holds my hand. He won't let go. "You can do it. Just take a step."

This is also a picture of who Mat is. If there's anyone I've known who will whisper into the darkness of the random rooftop you've gotten yourself stuck on, it's Mat. Over and over in the pages of this book, you can hear that same sentiment. "You can do it. Just take a step."

Mat has been my mentor and friend for years. Mat and Aimee have never given up on me, even when I was bitter or avoidant or running full speed into a brick wall. That's how I know what he has to say has the power to change the course of your life. He's already changed the course of mine.

So I hope you let his words challenge you, refresh you, and help you get out of bed in the morning to tackle a new season. I hope you let Mat be a guide, to remind you that the path ahead of you is beautiful and important. And when he says, "You can do it," I pray God gives you the courage to believe him.

So let me introduce you to one of my favorite people in the world – Mathu Thomason. I have a feeling you two will be great friends.

Debby Hanks

Introduction

Thank you so much for taking the time to read the introduction. I have a little confession to make. I usually skip the introduction and go straight to the first chapter. Forgive me.

Writing this book has been more about obedience than anything else. I felt like God told me to write a book about four years ago, and since I am such an obedient person, I waited until now to write it. At first I didn't think I could physically write a book. I thought maybe a couple of people could transcribe some of my teachings (thanks, Deb and Toni) or interview me and turn all of those random thoughts into a book. I thought it was the only way I was ever going to pull this off.

I tried that route for a few months. It seemed like a great idea at first, but things slowed down and then eventually it all died. I forget how far we made it, but it wasn't more than a couple of half-finished chapters. Fast forward to Spring 2016 in Cape Town. I was driving my car down Old Boyes Drive (I don't expect you to know where that is), knowing that eventually I was going to have to write something. I was pleading with God to help me, because I couldn't do it. I was quite emotional. The very thought of writing had become overwhelming to me.

The next day my friend Debby told me she wanted to help me write again. In fact, she was going to fly from the U.S. to South Africa and live with us for three months while I wrote the book. In that moment, a massive weight lifted off of me. I knew the book was actually going to get written this time. I didn't know how. I didn't know what it was about. But I knew it would eventually be finished.

Over the next few months, before Debby arrived from the States, I started to believe I could write this book with my own hands. At first, my mind was convinced that she would have to take my thoughts and type them into something coherent, but as I prayed about it more, I discovered that I would have to write it. It was a total surprise to me (and Debby and my wife, Aimee). But here I am, typing out these very words. No one is holding my hand. What seemed to be impossible is happening right before my eyes. I hear the Lost Boys saying, "You're doing it, Peter (sorry, random *Hook* reference)!"

I'm not convinced I will say anything new in this book. (Side note: maybe we try too hard to say "new" things.) (Side note for the side note: throughout the book I will do weird little things like "side notes." You'll get used to it.) What I might do is say some old things in a new way. In fact, I would be happy if this book was just a really thoughtful re-gift. You know, a gift you received a few birthdays/Christmases ago, and you pass it on because you don't have the money to buy anything new. There is a chance you won't suspect this book is a re-gift, and you'll think I'm the most thoughtful and creative gift giver you've ever met. That works for me.

I will try my hardest not to sound too smart (which should be relatively easy for me) and to engage with you on a personal level. My wife says I am at my best when I'm able to sit down and talk with people face to face. My hope is that when you read this book, it feels like you're having a conversation with me. It could be that we're at a coffee shop, just chillin' in my living room, or on a road trip together. Wherever it is, I hope you can hear in the tone of my voice that I care deeply about who you are as an individual. The whole point of me writing this book is for you to know how awesome you really are.

I am not an expert. I'm not writing a book because I have it all figured out. In fact, the older I get the less I know. (I have found it's quite an amazing thing to realize how little you know.) I'm still struggling to implement the things we will talk about in this book. Each chapter has presented me with its own set of tests and trials (just ask my wife). As you read, understand that we are all on a journey, myself included, and we haven't yet reached our destination.

For this part of the journey, let's just travel side by side for awhile. I'll do most of the talking. I apologize for that. I promise it won't take too long, if you promise to never ask, "Are we there yet?" If you want, we can even stop for snacks along the way (beef jerky, Doritos, maybe a Snickers bar?). Hopefully by the end you'll be inspired to write a book of your own or to reignite some other dream that has slowly started to fade from memory.

Maybe we'll never meet in "real life" and have that face to face conversation, but at least we will have shared something. And that's reason enough for me to write.

Part 1

Who Are We?

1

My Story

There are a few reasons I wanted to start this book off with my story. Firstly, one of the things I value most in my life is transparency, and I believe when we are transparent we break down the walls between us. I don't want any walls between us. Cool? Secondly, I wanted to make sure that you knew I was a normal person. Sometimes we put authors in a different category to ourselves. A higher category. I just wanted to assure you that I am a weird, slightly nerdy, sports fan from a really small town in Idaho. I probably look and act just like someone you know. Well maybe I'm slightly weirder than someone you know, but you get the picture. Thirdly, in order to start something, you need to start somewhere. Most people think their "somewhere" has to be some beautiful idyllic utopia when, in fact, anywhere will do.

It all started in the town of Grangeville, Idaho on January 2nd, 1980. Now, I'm actually not from

Grangeville, but the town I lived closest to, Craigmont, was so small it didn't have a hospital (yeah, that small...500 people small). So my parents (Shawn and Deanne) were forced to drive over thirty miles to bring me into the world. Maybe that's why I love road trips.

I was raised in a single-wide trailer in the woods a few miles outside of Craigmont. My childhood was spent in the forest with my brother Caleb. My mom's favorite line was, "Go outside and play!" So we did. (This is probably what kept her sane all those years.) We played with cars in the dirt, we climbed trees, we fought, we built forts, and we ran and ran and ran. I still feel most at home when I am in rural areas. Places where the air smells sweet and there are far more animals than people.

By the time I was twelve there were seven of us living in that two bedroom, single-wide trailer: my parents, my brother and I, and "the kids." We called them "the kids" because the three youngest siblings (Megn, Seth, and Caiti) were eight, ten, and twelve years younger than I was, which created two distinct sibling cultures. In some ways being the oldest was like being an uncle. "The kids" were so much younger that I never was able to connect with them on a friend level while I was living at home. I spent most of my time protecting them, disciplining them, or trying to teach them something. They taught me about patience and sacrifice. We've since become very close. I have always been close with Caleb, but I have a unique friendship with each of my siblings now. It's something I am so grateful for and will never take for granted.

My parents had the privilege of sleeping on a hide-a-bed (sleeper-couch) in the living room for the final eight years of my time at home. (When I think of my definition of love, it is heavily influenced by this fact.) I mean, really, who sleeps on a bed that you pull out of a couch for eight years? You have to either enjoy pain and be slightly crazy or be the most selfless people on the planet. It turns out it is a little of both (just kidding, Mom).

I remember watching TV on the floor in front of their bed. They would tell me to go to my room. I would try to stall by saying, "Hold on, I'm stretching." It never worked.

Throughout my entire upbringing, I never identified myself as poor. I knew that my friends had more money than we did, but I never felt different. I think part of the reason for that was my parents' outlook on life. They never talked or acted like we were poor. Even as our house began to fall apart, they always focused less on the things we didn't have and more on the things we did have. They just made it work. Who knows, if we would have had more, maybe we would have loved less.

In junior high and high school, I was a bit of a troublemaker. I always had more potential and attitude than follow-through and discipline. My most developed gift was my stubbornness, and I used it to devastating effect. Needless to say, I had quite a few "talks" with teachers, coaches, and principals. I even managed to get myself kicked off a couple of sports teams. Good times. I definitely thought too much about girls, cared too much about what people thought, and didn't care enough about how my actions affected others. I was basically a model student.

During high school, two life altering things happened to me. First, during a week of summer camp, I realized that I was called to ministry. Now did I know fully what that meant? No. Did all of my habits and attitudes change overnight? No. Was I a little terrified? Yes. All I can tell you is that I knew I was supposed to serve Him. Second, I had a dream that I was teaching a classroom full of kids. I don't remember a lot of my dreams, so when I do remember them (especially one as vivid as this one), I pay attention.

After I graduated, I moved three hours north to Coeur d'Alene, Idaho (CDA) to go to college and study to be a teacher (you know, because of the dream I told you about in the previous paragraph). I actually did quite a bit better in college than in high school. (Side note: it's amazing how much more effective we are at things when we know why we are doing them, even if our why is kind of abstract and difficult to explain to other people.) I started serving as a youth leader at my church's youth ministry, playing on the youth worship team, and I even played drums in a mildly successful Christian band called the Idahomies. Yes, you read that right. The Idahomies.

The highlight of my first couple of years in CDA was meeting a really cool redhead named Aimee. She became my best friend. After I graduated college, I married that really cool redhead and immediately started my career as a teacher. I substitute taught for a couple of months before I got my first gig at a private Christian school in the area.

Aimee and I had our first child, Kindle, just a year later. I assumed that this was the start of a very stable and somewhat comfortable married life. Right. Two months after my daughter was born the school closed its doors, and I was out of a job. So there I was, staring at this equation. $X = \text{infant} + \text{bills} - \text{job}$ (solve for X), and I'm horrible at algebra!

I spent the summer playing with my daughter. Maybe this was my way of ignoring my algebra homework, but I loved it! She had this swing that I would sit beside, and we would just have the best conversations. Goo goo, boo boo, gah gah, and other words that cannot be spelled. To be honest, I was a smidge stressed about the future. But man, I wouldn't have traded that time with Kindle for anything. She was perfect, just like her mom. I had known love before, but those first few months with Kindle taught me about a different kind of love.

That same summer, I turned down the perfect teaching position at another private school in town because I couldn't shake the feeling that God was saying, "No." It felt like the Holy Spirit was sitting on my heart, which is a strange sensation. At the time, I figured something better was just around the corner. (Something I have learned since then is that our definition of "better" almost never lines up with God's definition of "better.") I entered autumn with no prospects of ending my unemployed status, ever increasing stress levels, and an ever decreasing bank balance.

I was beginning to get desperate when September rolled around. Up until that point I had been fairly prideful about what I was willing to do. I had told Aimee multiple times that having a degree meant I didn't have to work at McDonald's. She wasn't impressed.

I was still holding out for God's "better" opportunity when a man named Bill approached me after Sunday service. He asked if I had found anything yet, and I said, "No." He asked if I wanted to come and pick up trash at his job sites (he was a general contractor), and I just knew I had to say yes. Did I want to pick up trash? No, but apparently God wanted me to.

For the next sixteen months I worked on all of Bill's job sites. What started out as trash pick-up turned into shoveling gravel, which turned into driving a dump truck, which turned into hanging doors, which turned into framing, which turned into driving machinery, which turned into laying tile, which turned into more things than I can remember right now. My time in construction was humbling, but it also built my confidence. I learned that no job was too small for me, but I also learned that no job was too big for me. It was a beautifully painful experience that changed me in so many wonderful and profound ways. I still refer to it as my Bible school, my theological training. God helped me to kill the man I thought I was and to awaken the man that had been slumbering inside of me.

Just when I was starting to get comfortable with my role as a construction worker, my brother Caleb called. The same brother that I ran around in the woods with as a kid had since become the youth pastor at the church we were attending. He was calling to let me know the church was looking for a children's pastor. He told me I should apply for the position. My response was, "Uh, no, not interested, but thanks for calling, Bro." To my dismay, he called again a week later. Come on, just apply!" I still didn't really want to do it, but I said, "Ok, fine!" A month later, on my 28th birthday, I was a children's pastor.

In nineteen months I had morphed from a teacher to a manual laborer to a pastor. It was kind of a crazy ride. There was a point during those nineteen months that I told God, "Ok, I'll do whatever You want me to do." Up until that point in my life I had always given Him criteria that He had to meet in order for me to do "whatever." "I'll do whatever You want as long as it isn't _____." Or, "I'll do whatever You want as long as I get _____." The Holy Spirit had squeezed that old way of thinking out of my brain. I told God, "If you want me to work construction for the rest of my life, I'll do it." I was serious. I had been humbled enough to realize that any job in His Kingdom was a job worth having.

The humbling process continued for the next six and a half years as God taught me how to pastor, how to lead, how to listen, how to follow, when to shut up, when to speak, and when to just get out of the way. It seemed like every year of pastoring brought with it a new challenge and a new set of fears to overcome. Who would have thought I was afraid of so many things? I would love to take the time to catalogue all of my mistakes for you, but that book would be so long you wouldn't read it anyway. Let's just assume that I tried my best to learn from each of them. Only God and my wife know if I truly did.

Toward the end of 2012, Aimee (the beautiful and freakishly kind redhead) and I found out we were pregnant with our second child. We had been praying and trying for another baby for six years with only a promise to hold onto. I won't lie, we probably lost heart a few times during those years, but God wouldn't let us forget His promise. I'll never forget the night that Aimee told me she was pregnant. I was in total shock. We were sitting on the coach, and I just kept staring straight ahead and saying, "What? No way!" The little man we had been waiting for was finally on his way.

When True arrived in August of 2013, we were two months away from our first family mission trip. I had been asked to work with a team of missionaries in South Africa for a couple weeks, so I figured why not bring the whole family. We had to hold up True's head for his passport photo because he wasn't strong enough yet. I wish you could see that picture. So tiny, so cute. I still can't believe we actually flew to the other side of the world with a two month old. (Side note: it was awesome!)

As our plane touched down in Cape Town I knew something was different about this trip, and it only intensified as we drove through the city to our hostel. Aimee and I had talked about moving to different places in the world, but I don't think we were ever serious. We had just bought our first house, Kindle was starting 2nd grade, I had a secure position as an associate pastor at our church, and we had an infant. Generally, this is a list that screams, "Don't do anything drastic! Just play it safe!"

But I couldn't get this crazy idea out of my head. Again, it felt like the Holy Spirit was sitting on my heart, and a voice not quite like a voice but more like a shimmering thought with wings was saying, "I want you to move here." I wasn't sure how Aimee would react when I told her, but it turned out she was feeling the same thing. Now, if you haven't already figured it out, I'm the crazy one in this family. So if my sweet, settled, content wife also thinks that God is asking us to move to the other side of the world...well, stuff just got real.

As soon as we got back to the States I set up a meeting with Gary, our pastor. I told him the whole story and asked him to pray about it. A week later he told me he thought it was God (even though he would have preferred that we stayed). We immediately began preparing to move. It is a strange process when you begin to boil down your American sized life to the point where it will fit into a few pieces of luggage. You learn a lot about what is really important to you and what you had just been keeping around for a rainy day. We sold everything but our house, some boxes of memories, and seven suitcases that would travel with us to Cape Town. Looking back, I can't believe Aimee and I survived it. There were times when we were fighting over whether to keep some old t-shirt or not. Seriously.

By the end of September 2014, we were on a British Airways plane with an eight year old, a one year old, and seven suitcases with our lives crammed into them.

How did I get from Craigmont to Cape Town, from Idaho to South Africa? I sit writing this in a coffee shop just over the mountain from my flat in suburban Cape Town, and I still struggle to answer that question.

There isn't anything special about me (unless you ask my wife or mother). I don't have a genius level IQ (as I am sure you can tell from my writing), I have never taken performance enhancing drugs (to my knowledge), and I haven't figured out a cheat code for life. I just said yes, over and over again. Life, when you simplify it, is just one small decision after another. I suppose you could say it is like a series of switches, on for yes and off for no. My hope is that by the time you finish this book you won't be afraid to flip a few more of your switches into the yes position.

2

Who We Are

When I sit down and talk to people, the conversation will inevitably land on how they view themselves and how that view affects their decision making. To be honest, most of us (including myself) have no idea who we are. So much of what we believe about ourselves is based on the input of others, and generally that input is based on how they see themselves rather than on how they see us. The girl that tells you that you're ugly because she doesn't feel pretty, or the boy that tells you that you're stupid because he needs to feel smart. The words "ugly" and "stupid" are just words, but words can be transformed into weapons when we believe them. And if words can be turned into weapons based on what we believe, then what we believe becomes paramount in the fight for our identity.

In my own life, I tend to be my own worst enemy. For years I believed I was unqualified because I viewed myself through a lens I had constructed. It was based on my own biases toward success, failure, value, intelligence, etc. It took me years to realize that my lens needed to be broken and reformed in order to see myself correctly. This chapter is all about breaking our lenses, and allowing God to reform them so that our true identity comes into focus.

BEFORE YOU WERE FORMED

If we believe that we were created by God, then we should also believe that the very essence of who we are was birthed in His divine mind before we were formed. This means that before we were made flesh, we existed as a thought. That thought existed like a blueprint in the mind of The Creator before a breath entered our lungs, before He began to attach muscle and sinew to our bones. It was a blueprint for gifts, talents, and personality.

"I knew you before I formed you in your mother's womb. Before you were born I set you apart and appointed you as my prophet to the nations (Jeremiah 1:5)." In two short sentences God reveals His divine plan for Jeremiah, but he also gives us insight into the way He deals with all of us. This is such a foundational verse for me. I go back to it over and over when I feel unqualified or unworthy. I believe it reveals three extremely important truths that must make the journey from our head to our heart.

First, God declares that He knew us before He formed us. Ok, maybe some of you are like, "Uh yeah, Mat, God knows everything." That's fair, but let me say this. We don't live our lives like He does know everything. We live like our qualifications and suitability rest squarely on our shoulders. As if God is in heaven saying, "I hope that they figure this out soon, because if they don't, I won't be able to use them." This might be news to you, but your life isn't a job interview. Jesus died, so you're hired. We spend too much time trying to convince God that we are worthy and not enough time convincing the world that He is worthy. If He knew us before we were formed, then He knew us before we ever did a "good" or "bad" thing. He knew us before we made all of those mistakes, and He still chose us.

Second, He says, "Before you were born I set you apart..." This means that He made you special. There is no heavenly assembly line that just churns out one identical, boring piece after another. You are special. The unique mix of gifts and talents He put inside of you is not an accident. You were not created with a long list of flaws that must be fixed for you to be ready for use. You are gold. And no matter where you find gold, whether in the mud, in the dump, or in the sewer, it never loses its value. No matter where you find yourself, all you have to do is let Jesus clean you, and He will reveal what has been inside of you the entire time.

Finally, before you were born He appointed you. I like to use the term pre-qualified. You were pre-qualified by Him to do amazing things. You were literally designed for greatness. Each of us needs to grapple with this truth. You can't just know it like you know Jesus is the answer to every Sunday school question. You have to know it like you know an apple will fall to the ground if you drop it. It has to become like a law that governs your universe, "I was designed for greatness." You have to know that God didn't make a mistake when He made you. No matter the obstacle, you were appointed to overcome it.

A LITTLE HAMMER

Let's pretend for a moment that you and I and all of humankind are tools in an oversized toolbox. Some of us are saws, some are pliers, some are screwdrivers, and some of us are hammers. The toolbox holds a myriad of tools of all shapes, sizes, and functions. Outside the toolbox there are various jobs to be done. There are boards to be cut, nails to be hammered, and screws to be turned. There is more than enough work for everyone.

Our biggest problem as tools isn't that we were poorly made. Instead, it is that we don't have any idea what we are. Apparently there aren't any mirrors in the toolbox, or if there are we are too scared to look in them. Parents tell their children stories about the wisdom of staying in the toolbox and the tragedies that befall the foolish few who dare to venture beyond the walls. Everyone knows that "the box" (local slang) is the safest place to be.

Let's say that you are a lonely little hammer tucked in the back corner of the toolbox. You haven't looked into any of the mirrors either, so you have no idea that you're a hammer. You have dreamed of leaving the toolbox and trying your hand at a few jobs, but where do you begin? You've heard the stories of other tools that left only to return broken and bitter. Despite that, there is still a small voice inside of you that keeps whispering, "Go for it."

One day, you stir up enough courage to leave the toolbox. There you are, hopping along (because hammers hop), when you come across a screw sticking up out of a piece of wood beside the path. "Well," you say, "here goes nothing." You take your best swing, and the screw snaps in half. Everything that you feared is coming true. Even though you have never looked in a mirror, you now know that you are the worst screwdriver in the history of the toolbox. "I knew it! I should have never left the box." You spend the next few months telling everyone that you are a broken screwdriver. You try to drown out the small voice that won't stop reminding you. "Go for it."

Just when you think your life has returned to normal, an old tool hops into the box. He is covered in dings and scars, but he also wears something that you haven't seen in awhile – a smile. You see him the next day telling stories with a large crowd gathered around him. You wait patiently until he is finished and everyone has shuffled away. You take a deep breath and hop over to ask him a question, but before you can form the words he says, "What's your story?"

You go on to tell him about your decision to venture outside the box, your journey, and the revelation of your brokenness as a screwdriver. The old tool nods while he listens, but the look in his eyes tells you that he doesn't quite believe you. He stops you mid sentence and confidently states, "You look like a hammer to me." This guy has probably taken one too many hits to the head, but when he speaks it sounds just like that small voice inside of you.

After a night of restless sleep filled with dreams of adventures outside the box, you roll out of bed. You scan the streets, but the old tool is nowhere to be found. Someone tells you they saw him leave early that morning. You hop to the edge of the box and look toward the east hoping to catch a glimpse of him before he fades out of sight. Then, like a ray of sunlight, that small voice pushes itself through your cloud of doubt. "Go for it!"

With more fear in your heart than you care to admit, you jump over the wall of the toolbox and start your journey east. The charred landscape is more desolate than you remember, which only adds to your anxiety. As the path begins to climb in elevation, something off to your left catches your attention. There stands a nail, defiant in the morning light. The words of the old tool flash through your mind. "You look like a hammer to me." Fighting through the fear, pain, and disappointment of your past, you take a swing and discover that you were a perfectly good hammer all along.

So what is the moral of this story? We can learn a few things from the little hammer about our identity. The first is that we can't draw conclusions about our identity or value from the success or failure of our actions. In fact, we derive far too much value from outcomes. The value or worth of a hammer is based on the materials that were used to craft it and the reputation of the craftsman, not on the number of nails it has or has not driven. Use does not create value, it reveals it. Your identity and value are defined by Him, not by what you do.

Second, we can learn a lot about our identity by not being afraid to try things. We are all intimately acquainted with our phobias, but our strengths are strangers. What if one of the ways that we discovered our strengths was by doing things that scared us? What if you had to leave the toolbox for the fullness of who you are to be revealed? I believe we were created to be adventurers. We were created to explore the uncharted regions, both outside and inside of us. Clues about your identity are waiting to be discovered. "Go for it!"

Third (this will serve as an epilogue to the story of the little hammer), as our identity becomes clearer to us, what we once viewed as an obstacle transforms into an opportunity. When the little hammer approached that first nail he was petrified, "What if it happens again? What if I truly am broken?" But after that first nail was driven, every nail he approached after that could not create the same level of fear in him that the first nail had created. In fact, he began to notice that the more nails he encountered, the more his fear and anxiety were replaced by joy and anticipation. Imagine a world where the things that frighten you today excite you tomorrow. That world is waiting for you.

MAYBE YOU WERE MADE FOR THIS

I want to end this chapter with a story that I find myself sharing more and more as I realize its importance. It's a moment that has had a profound effect on me and has subsequently shaped the way I look at myself and any challenges I face.

About five years ago I was invited to teach a team of missionaries in Croatia. I had never been asked to do anything like that in my entire life. So, of course, I played it cool. "Sure, let me check my schedule. Hmmm, ok, I think I can squeeze it in."

I asked my brother Seth (one of "the kids") to travel with me because I thought it would be fun to experience Europe together. Also, having one or both of my brothers around keeps me relaxed and normal (when you read normal, think weird). To this day, I send him random texts saying, "Remember when we did _____ in Croatia? Good times." Anyway, back to the story.

The team I was tasked with teaching consisted of photographers from various nations who had been traveling around the globe documenting injustice. They had already traveled to like a million countries (maybe a little less than that), and their passports had more stamps than a post office. The stories of their journeys and the people they had met along the way were inspiring. I stopped just short of having them sign autographs (well, maybe just one or two).

I remember sitting at the front of the room in our first meeting thinking, "What am I doing here? I'm not qualified for this. They should be teaching me. Lord, seriously, what am I doing here?" Maybe I was expecting Him to say, "Ummm, I don't know, son. This wasn't my idea." Instead, His thoughts invaded mine and this question elevated itself above the dull mechanical hum of my brain. "What are YOU doing here?" He had returned my question to me, but instead of it dripping with desperation and self pity, it was calm and full of confidence. His thoughts continued, "Why did I send you? Maybe you were made for this." He had me cornered. I could either continue whining or shut up and believe. I chose the latter.

Something changed the moment I chose to believe. I spent the next two weeks pastoring, counseling, and teaching that team of missionaries. In the process I discovered that the challenge that had been placed before me wasn't an obstacle, it was an invitation. God was inviting me to become what He had already created me to be.

Take a minute and think of the challenges you are facing, think about the obstacles in your path that seem insurmountable. They might look like a seven foot, four hundred pound giant with a voice that sounds like an avalanche and a sword taller than you. Maybe the giant is laughing at you right now, and you're thinking, "What am I doing here?" But, maybe, just maybe, you have five smooth stones in your shepherd's bag and a sling in your hand. Maybe you were made for this.

PART 2

Why We Don't

3

I'm Afraid

Welcome to the club. We're all afraid. This might sound ridiculous, but I was afraid to write this book. For over four years, I put it off in hopes that God would miraculously write it for me. I used to get anxious just thinking about it. It wasn't until three months ago that God finally convinced me that I, the kid that hated English class, could actually write a book.

Even as I write this paragraph, I have to tell myself, "You've got this. Just write." My fear kept me from considering the possibility I would enjoy writing. I assumed it would be like strapping myself to a medieval torture device or like being forced to watch all seven seasons of *Gilmore Girls* (sorry, honey).

I was convinced I would have to suffer through each page as I "willingly" submitted to God's plan. (Side note: Sometimes, doing what God asks can be enjoyable! Who knew?) To my surprise, I love it! Seriously. I'm only five thousand words into this book, and I'm already thinking of writing another.

What about you? What's standing in your way? What are you afraid of? In this chapter we'll talk about fear — what it is and what it does to us. Fear is at the heart of almost every excuse on our excuse pile. It is the power that snuffs out dreams and imprisons the adventurer inside of us. If we can slay this beast, then literally anything is possible.

TRUST ME

Imagine that you are an only child to the most wonderful set of parents the world has ever known. You live in a quiet house, on a quiet street corner, in a quiet town. Directly across from your quiet house is an empty lot. It has been empty for exactly one more summer than you have been alive. It is overgrown with weeds and the types of flowers that only five year olds pick for their moms.

One day, your father pulls you aside and asks if you would like to collect some soil from the empty lot across the street. He has a bit of a green thumb and wants to pot a lavender plant. He hands you a bag and a shovel, looks into your eyes and says, "Listen. Don't worry. The weeds aren't poisonous." You respond, "OK, Dad," and head out the door.

As you skip down your front steps, you hear kids down the street singing, "The weeds are poison, the weeds are poison!" You look up and a man with a super official uniform begins to pound a sign into the ground that reads, "CAUTION! POISONOUS WEEDS!" A memory flashes into your mind from a conversation you overheard at the mall last week, "Well, you know, I've been hearing a lot of bad things about those weeds."

In your heart you come to the conclusion, "I think I misunderstood what Dad said." So you slowly turn around, drop the bag and shovel, and sprint back into the quiet house on the corner.

Tragically, this scenario plays out in our lives on a regular basis. We receive purpose, direction, and encouragement from our Father, but external influences immediately come to cancel out the very words of life that caused us to skip out the front door in the first place. We try to justify our actions with phrases like "Better safe than sorry." But we're just denying the fact that something spiritually significant has occurred. We have made a decision to trust in something or someone other than our Father.

When we choose to fear, we are choosing to give trust to someone, or something, other than God. When God says, "Fear not," what He really means is, "Trust me." For example, my fear in writing this book was ultimately trusting my own estimation of my abilities more than God's. God says, "Write a book." And my response is, "I think you have the wrong guy."

Don't worry, I'm in good company. Moses argued, "I can't speak." Jeremiah whined, "I'm too young." Gideon said, "I am the least." Honestly, this has got to be the most frustrating thing for God. He takes the time to create, position, and empower us for His purpose, and we respond with, "Are You sure?"

Trust, like most things, can't be in two places at once. We can't trust our Father's words, "The weeds aren't poisonous," while at the same time trusting the words, "CAUTION! POISONOUS WEEDS!" We have to choose one or the other, but we seldom choose based on faith (the evidence of things not seen). Instead, we choose based on what we see. We trust our circumstances and our apparent lack of ability more than His judgment. Until our Father's words become more real to us than the caution sign across the street, we will continually find ourselves running back to the quiet house on the corner.

EPIC FAIL

For most of my life nothing has scared me more than failing. I remember discovering in fourth grade that I wasn't fast enough to beat my friend Aaron at our mad minute math quizzes and immediately deciding that I didn't care anymore. "Who cares!?" Of course, I cared. But if I kept trying and finishing second then what was the point? Even at nine years old I knew it was better to give up than face my fear of failing.

Most of us are that way. We find it far more appealing to quit – or worse, to never even try – than to endure the pain of failure. Part of the reason for this struggle is the belief that our value comes from our success. If our value increases or decreases based on our level of personal success, then the odds are high that we will fear failure.

The problem with this line of thinking is that "success" is based on a fluid definition that changes depending on who or what we are listening to. Let's say my Dad is a banker, and according to him, banking is the pinnacle of human existence. "Son, if you aren't a banker, well, you're nobody." His father was a banker, his grandfather was a banker that was born inside of a bank vault, and you get the idea. As his son, my definition of "success" is heavily skewed by his opinions on "success." If I become a teacher, I'm a failure. If I become a nurse, I'm a failure. I can't be me; I can only be a banker or a failure. What do I do?

My hope is that, as individuals, we would begin to redefine these terms that have ruled our world for so long. What if success wasn't defined by Hollywood, society, or culture? What if we didn't have to compare ourselves to others to discover how much or how little we are worth? What if instead of chasing "success" and fearing failure, we spent our life chasing dreams and fearing God? What if "success" was defined more by who we are and less by what we do?

In Proverbs 24:16 it says, "The godly may trip seven times, but they will get up again." In our minds, we equate tripping or falling with failure, but, apparently, we can trip and still be godly. "But, Mat, don't we have to be perfect to be godly? I thought we could never make mistakes." Sorry, no, becoming more like God isn't about eliminating failure or mistakes. It's about what we do after we trip and fall. The only way we can fail is if we never try to run. Don't let the fear of failure stop you from running with the freedom that Jesus purchased for you. Run, trip, fall, trip again, but whatever you do, don't stop running.

We tend to look at life like it's a machine filled with gears, rods, springs, and gaskets. If we take care of it, keep it well lubricated, and don't push it beyond its manufacturing limits, then it will produce what we need from it. Machines need a proper maintenance schedule and the right oil, or there will be problems. Machines are so complicated that we need specialized mechanics to work on them.

When we look at life in this way, we create a world where mistakes are impossible. In a mechanical world, nearly every mistake could lead to failure. We become our worst critics. We overanalyze every move and second guess every decision, until eventually we fear making decisions altogether (sound familiar?). Instead of putting the wrong oil in the engine, we decide it's safer not to put oil in at all.

What if there weren't equations to memorize or diagrams to follow? What if, instead of a perfectly engineered machine, life was more like art? If we approach our lives like a painting, then our mistakes are just part of the "artistic process." Maybe one of the brushstrokes doesn't look exactly like it should, or the color turned out just a little bit off. The only way that we can redeem the fumbled brushstrokes that dot the canvas of our life is to continue to paint.

I have a friend that's an artist (that sounds so cool when I read it out loud). She lived with my wife and me for a few months, and we got to witness her creating on a regular basis. She is the type of artistic talent that I put into the magic category. When she sketches or paints, my brain literally has no idea how she does it. Magic!

One of the many magical things that she does is she takes random doodles and turns them into complete works of art. For instance, if I took a chicken, a pencil, and a piece of paper, and locked all three in a room, then took whatever was left from that crazy dance party and handed it to her, she would be able to turn it into something that would force a "Whoa!" out of you.

Whenever I think of her amazing gift, I think of how God works in our lives. Romans 8:28 says, "...God causes everything to work together for the good of those that love God and are called according to His purpose for them." God is telling us that even if we end up scribbling on our canvas, even if we make a mess, He is going to make it good if we allow Him. What better incentive do we need to overcome our fear of failure than to hear, from God himself, that He will use our errant brushstrokes to create a stunning masterpiece?

WHAT WILL THEY THINK?

There are so many different types of fear we could address in this chapter. I chose to talk about the fear of failure and the fear of man because they are the two giants that I struggle with the most. I've always tricked myself into thinking I didn't care what people thought, but most of the time, deep down, I wanted validation and acceptance. Of course I would never let anyone know that, but it's true.

Again, to use the writing of this book as an example, one of the scariest things for me was what people would think about it. Would they think I was just saying things that have already been said before? Would they think I was pretending to be more intelligent than I actually was? Would they think I was a joke? These are real thoughts that passed through my mind, and I had to consciously overcome each one. Honestly, I've had to overcome them every day since I started.

It's nearly impossible to serve someone with a pure heart if you care what they think about you. When we serve with an underlying desire for validation or acceptance, we set up a scenario where our service transforms from a gift to a transaction. We begin to change who, what, where and when we serve in order to receive the maximum return on our investment. We can even open a door to frustration and bitterness when our "gift" isn't received in the way we had hoped. When we allow the fear of man to pollute our motives, we end up either starting something for the wrong reasons or not starting anything at all.

In order to push myself over the starting line, I had to remind myself (and listen to the reminders of my wife) of my motivation for writing the book in the first place. I want to serve people. I dream of people understanding their value, overcoming their fears, silencing the critical voices in their heads, and embarking on the adventure of a lifetime. I knew I'd struggle to see any of those dreams come to fruition if I didn't overcome my own fear of man. First, what the person in front of me thought as I spoke. Second, what the room full of missionaries thought as I taught. And finally, what you are thinking now as you read this book. I had to learn to move past those fears in order to serve.

We all have the ability to silence the critical voices that bombard our minds because there is one voice that rises above the rest. The voice of truth. The voice that created, called, and empowered us. We can choose to believe His words of validation and acceptance or choose to believe the voices that want to corner us in our fear and indecision. God can't do that part for us. The choice is ours.

WHO CARES?

Comparison is another trap that I fall into that directly relates to my fears. Instead of going to God to reassure me when I doubt myself, I let my fear of failure/man lead me to compare myself to others. If I can find someone "worse" than me, then I can go on. But if I find someone "better" than me, it's time to give up. This is what kept me from trying my best at math in fourth grade, the thought that, "I will never be better than Aaron. So, who cares, I'm done trying."

I assumed I had come a long way since fourth grade, but a couple weeks back I was browsing through Amazon, looking for books that were similar to what I was thinking of writing, when I stumbled across one (I'm not going to tell you which one) that sounded very similar. As I stared at my computer screen, I felt the fear rising up in me. The author was definitely smarter than I was, he had tons more experience, and he even had a foreword written by Bob

Goff. (I think my foreword will be written by my Mom.) I thought, "What is the point of writing a book?"

I started to use my new found status as a second class citizen to my disadvantage. "The world doesn't need another book like this. I should just tell people to read his book." The fear of failure and of man had led me to a place where I was comparing myself to some random author, and I was losing in every category.

The words I used in fourth grade to signal my surrender were the same words I used in that moment to shake off the self pity and start typing. Who cares!? Who cares if it's been done before! Who cares if I feel unqualified! Who cares if I'll never be the Steph Curry of authors, I'm still going to shoot!

What I want to know is, are you going to shoot? Are you going to decide today to stare down the fear of failure, the fear of man's opinions, and the lies that you believe about yourself, and just take a chance? Who cares if you're so scared you're shaking? Who cares if you make a mistake? Who cares if things don't turn out perfect? Who cares if everyone thinks you're crazy? Take the ball, take a breath, and just shoot.

4

I'm Unqualified

The phrase "I'm unqualified" has flashed through my mind on multiple occasions throughout my life, and until about five years ago I believed it nearly every time I thought it. The enlightening moment I had in Croatia (the one I told you about in Chapter 2) changed those words from an overpowering scream to an annoying whisper. Now, because of that Croatian revelation (that sounds pretty cool), I'm more likely to believe the words "I'm qualified."

But what does it mean to be qualified? Most of us immediately imagine university degrees, vast experience, and glowing recommendations. When we say someone is qualified what we are really saying is they are fit for a job. Qualifications are great if you are advertising for a concert pianist, but what do you look for when you are trying to fill the position of world changer?

God certainly has His own set of qualifying criteria. In Jeremiah's case, God chose him for the position of Prophet to the Nations before he was formed. What criteria could Jeremiah have possibly fulfilled preconception? God "hired" him as a prophet before he could read. I mean, God can't use someone without a theological degree, right? (Side note: I am pro education. I was a teacher. So, don't think that I am saying getting a degree is evil, just do it for the right reasons.)

We humans try to control outcomes by controlling input. If we can weed out the unfit by forcing them to qualify for participation, then we think we can control the results of that participation. But our qualification system only gives us a false sense of security. There is nothing that we can do that will make us or anyone else fit for service in His Kingdom. Only God can do that. Until we release control of the process to Him, we're only fooling ourselves.

In this chapter we're going to look at examples of biblical characters who God considered qualified. We'll begin by examining the journey of a fisherman and his apparent lack of credentials.

THE FISHERMAN

"One day as Jesus was walking along the shore of the Sea of Galilee, he saw two brothers – Simon, also called Peter, and Andrew – throwing a net into the water for they fished for a living. Jesus called out to them, 'Come, follow me, and I will show you how to fish for people (Matthew 4:18-19).'"

Let's set the scene. Jesus isn't too far removed from being baptized, affirmed by a voice from heaven, and tested in the wilderness. He had taught a little in Galilee, but He knew that He required a group of people to witness His ministry and message and to broadcast it to the world after His earthly task was complete. Jesus is casually strolling along the banks of a lake when He spots two brothers fishing. So like only Jesus can do, He calls for them to leave their lives as fishermen and follow Him into the unknown.

OK, imagine yourself in Jesus' position. You are looking for men that will be the first leaders of your Church. They will be tasked with turning the world upside down through the preaching of the Gospel. You know you'll be spending the next three years walking, praying, and breaking bread with these people. You know that by the time you return to your Father in heaven they will need to be ready to do greater works than you have done. Then one of the first guys you come across is a fisherman named Simon. My guess is if you were in that place of authority, you might give Simon a polite wave and ask if the fish are biting. You certainly wouldn't invite him along.

I wouldn't even be looking at the edge of a lake. I would've been in the synagogues looking for the brightest and most charismatic young men in all of Israel. I would have been searching for the boys who had won every Bible quiz they had ever entered. I might even put on a competition called Israel's Got Talent and hold auditions that would eventually lead to me choosing a group of twelve handsome and ubertalented dudes (basically, the world's first boy band). I would take my time because this group can't be made up of just anybody. This assignment is too important to be left to the "unqualified."

Instead, Jesus (to everyone's surprise) called to Simon. A fisherman – and not just any fisherman, but a stubborn fisherman who had a tendency to speak and act before he thought. A fisherman that would go on to deny his relationship with Jesus on three separate occasions. Jesus decided this uneducated man from Galilee would help feed the five thousand, stand with Him on the Mount of Transfiguration, preach on the day of Pentecost, and lead the Acts Church as it spread the hope of Christ to the nations.

Don't get me wrong, I love Peter. He was passionate, bold, and fiercely loyal. He was so crazy that all it took for him to jump out of the boat was for Jesus to say, "Yes, come (Matthew 14:29)." He cut off a dude's ear (so intense!) to protect Jesus. He sprinted to the empty tomb when he heard the news of Jesus' resurrection. (Peter might have been a little out of shape because John got there first.) He was awesome, and he was normal!

That is my favorite part about Peter. He was so normal. He was like me. Just a random guy from a random town that responded to the call of Jesus. I wonder if on that first night as a follower, just before falling asleep next to his brother, he thought, "What am I doing here?" He had woken up that morning stressing about how he was going to provide for his family, and he fell asleep contemplating what Jesus meant by "fishers of men." He couldn't have grasped the enormity of what jumping out of his boat and swimming to shore would mean for his life or anticipated the overwhelming grace that he would be shown throughout his journey. Like me, he was probably still trying to figure out why Jesus picked him.

Peter's story might cause us to believe that God purposely picks the unqualified, but is that what's really happening here? Was Peter unqualified? Well, yes and no. By our standards he didn't have enough experience or education to be chosen. We would have told him, "Thank you, Peter, for applying, but we've decided to go with someone else." In contrast, Jesus knew Peter already had everything that was required because God had given it to him.

Peter himself wrote, "By His divine power, God has given us everything we need for living a godly life (2 Peter 1:3)." Peter had discovered something in his time with Jesus, something that he wanted to communicate to everyone that would come after him. The qualifications you need for service in the Kingdom have already been given to you. All that you need to do is jump out of the boat and follow.

THE EIGHTH SON

Like Peter, David seemed under qualified. He didn't tick all the boxes you would expect a future king to tick. Even Samuel, God's prophet, didn't expect David, and he certainly wouldn't have anticipated traveling to Bethlehem, to the house of Jesse. A king couldn't come from Bethlehem, could he?

Even if Samuel accepted the fact that a king could come from anywhere, he was still quite convinced that a king had a certain look. Someone that looked more like Saul, a head taller than the rest of the crowd. He was certain that the next king was Jesse's son Eliab as soon as he laid eyes on him, "Surely this is the Lord's anointed (1 Samuel 16:6)!" (Side note: How often are we drawn into this same type of thinking when we consider our own credentials? We think we know what a king or queen looks like, don't we? Maybe we're wrong?) God gently reminded Samuel, "The Lord doesn't see things the way you see them...the Lord looks at the heart (1 Samuel 16:7)."

Samuel was still pondering God's words as one by one the seven sons of Jesse walked in front of him, and one by one the Lord shook His head until none remained. "Then Samuel asked, 'Are these all the sons you have?' Jesse replied, 'There is still the youngest, but he is out in the fields watching the sheep and goats (1 Samuel 16:11).'" Maybe Jesse called David "the youngest" because he had forgotten David's name. Regardless, you get the impression that the little shepherd boy isn't on anyone's radar.

Let's recap. The seven sons of Jesse were paraded before Samuel, even though Jesse had eight sons. The eighth son is off taking care of the herds. The eighth son is so overlooked by everyone, including his own father, that he isn't even called in from the fields when a national celebrity comes to his house. This boy, the one who spends more time with animals than people, is the choice to succeed Saul as the next king of Israel. This is the guy? He isn't even the most qualified candidate in his own family.

I'm sure Samuel wanted to smack Jesse upside the head with his staff, but instead he said, "'Send for him at once...We will not sit down to eat until he arrives.' So Jesse sent for him...And the Lord said, 'This is the one; anoint him.' So as David stood there among his brothers, Samuel took the flask of oil he had brought and anointed David with oil. And the Spirit of the Lord came powerfully upon David from that day on (1 Samuel 16:11-13)."

Even though David outwardly looked like the most unqualified of his brothers, God had noticed something. It wasn't David's good looks, his sheep whispering abilities, or his stellar home school education. It wasn't his wealth, status, or reputation, for he had none of these things. God noticed his heart.

David is proof that greatness can come from the most dysfunctional family. God isn't concerned with where you came from or what you know, He is only concerned with your heart. If you can find a way to surrender it to Him, then nothing can stand in the way of His purposes for your life. Who knows? One day you might be king.

QUALIFICATION VS. PREPARATION

Both Peter and David's stories are perfect examples of the difference between qualification and preparation. Both were qualified, but neither were prepared. Peter had the ingredients of an apostle, but he needed three years of walking with Jesus to prepare him. David had the ingredients of a king, but he needed the bear, the lion, the giant, and the caves to prepare him.

We tend to confuse qualification and preparation. We assume we aren't qualified, so how can we respond to the call of God until we are? But the call of God is proof that we are qualified. It isn't qualification that we need. It's preparation. We need to get over ourselves just long enough to enter into that glorious, grace filled journey of growth called preparation.

Imagine you are baking a cake. You lay out all the ingredients on the counter in front of you. Eggs, salt, sugar, flour, butter, etc. Everything you need for a light and fluffy cake is before you. You start shoving handfuls of sugar, butter, and flour into your mouth. Tada! Cake! Right? Ok, maybe not. In order to get the cake you have been dreaming of, you need to prepare it. Combining the ingredients, mixing, and baking it in the oven are what transform that pile of random ingredients into a finished culinary masterpiece. That seems to be how God works with us.

When Jesus gazed across the surface of the lake at Simon, He knew inside that stinky fisherman were all the ingredients He needed to bake His apostle cake. All of Peter's passion, desire, loyalty, energy, and stubbornness just needed some time in the mixing bowl. So, Jesus invited him to follow. Peter's decision to surrender his will to Jesus is what initiated the preparation process. If Peter would have stayed in the boat, he would have remained a disjointed list of ingredients. Peter's potential to become a tasty baked delight would have always been there, but Peter's response to the call is what opened the door for Jesus to begin to sift and mix him.

David's preparation, on the other hand, started when he was still in the fields with the sheep and goats. David had no idea that the bear or the lion would lead to a Goliath, he was just protecting the flock. He could have run away and left those sheep to die, but he didn't. Each time he overcame his fears, the size of his adversary would increase, and with it his faith. As God turned up the heat, David had a choice to either resist or submit to the process. Even though all the ingredients for a king cake were there, David still had to face his fears and surrender to the heat of the oven.

God is the only one who knows what your random pile of ingredients can be turned into. Maybe it's a cake. Maybe it's a pie. Honestly, it doesn't matter right now. What matters is that you stop looking in the mirror, wishing you had the ingredients for greatness. The ingredients are in you. Your job is to trust that God is pleased with what He sees. Allow Him to have His way with your life and surrender your heart. He will finish what He started in you. He promised.

YOU DON'T HAVE TO PROVE IT

Before we move on to the next chapter, let's look at just one more story in the New Testament. Some time before Jesus called to Peter from the banks of the Sea of Galilee, we find Jesus in the Jordan River, where He had come to be baptized by His cousin, John. John is like, "What?! You can't be serious. Me?" But despite John's protests, he ultimately relents to Jesus' request.

As Jesus emerges from the water, a voice from heaven makes a declaration for all the world to hear, "This is my dearly loved son, who brings me great joy." Then Jesus was led by the Spirit into the wilderness to be tempted there by the devil. For forty days and forty nights he fasted there and became very hungry. During that time the devil came and said to Him, "If you are the Son of God, tell these stones to become loaves of bread.' But Jesus told him, 'No (Matthew 3:17-4:4)!'"

What a crazy story! Forty days without food. Seriously? I think I could have fought off the urge to turn rocks into bread, but if the devil would have said, "Turn these rocks into cheeseburgers," or "Turn these weeds into French fries," it would have been game over for me. Once I get a burger and fries on my mind all Scripture memorization goes out the window.

OK, try to forget about the food I just mentioned, and track with me. I want to focus on the difference between God's words spoken to Jesus and the devil's words. When the devil approached Jesus, he resorted to his usual line of questioning. In the garden it was, "Did God really say...?" In the wilderness it was, "If you are..." It seems like this is one of the devil's main tactics, turning statements of truth into questions of doubt. When God spoke to Jesus on his baptism day, it was with a clear statement of identity. "This is my dearly loved son." Jesus didn't have to wonder where He stood with His father. God made it perfectly clear.

This is the point where the devil tends to get really tricky. We get a little revelation of our identity (maybe not as dramatically as Jesus did), and we begin to walk in that new identity. We realize we are qualified or that we are good enough. But instead of just attacking that truth, the devil comes at us from a different angle. The same angle that he came at Jesus in the wilderness. He asks us to prove it.

"OK, if you are qualified to lead...prove it!" In one way or another we have all heard these words rolling around in our heads. It is this phrase that tends to drive a lot of people. It drove me for years. I tried to prove I was a man, to prove I was smart enough, to prove I was a hard worker, to prove I was worthy, etc. I spent years of my life trying to prove myself, and it was exhausting. (Side note: I believe so much of our striving and stress comes from this place of trying to prove it. Take some time to process your own motives, and ask yourself the question, "Am I trying to prove something?")

In the wilderness, Jesus faced the same pressure that you and I face every day. "If you are the son of God, prove it!" But because He knew who He was, without a doubt in His mind, He didn't have to answer any of the devil's challenges. He didn't have to dance to the devil's tune, because He had nothing to prove. I can just imagine the smile on Jesus' face as the devil tried harder and harder to trap Him, to get him to budge even a little, but Jesus was secure in who He was.

How much more restful would our lives be if we stopped trying to prove it? How much more peace would we live in if we stopped trying to make ourselves good enough and just lived as if we were already good enough? No matter what your dad says, or your friends say, or your teachers say, or society says, you don't have to prove a thing. So just relax, take a cue from the life of Jesus, and believe what your Father says about you.

It's all true, every word of it.

5

You Don't Know What I've Done

In all my years of mentoring, this is the number one excuse I hear. I tell the person sitting across from me all the things you've already read in the first few chapters of this book, which usually leads to a few nods of agreement. There could even be some tears shed, and then that look appears that only starts to form when a person realizes the truth. Then, right when I think it's all sinking in, I hear, "Mat, I appreciate what you're saying, and it makes perfect sense. But you don't know what I've done."

Let's be real. I've heard a lot of crazy stuff. I won't go into any detail, but there isn't much that surprises me anymore. It hasn't always been that way. There was definitely a time in my life, as a young follower of Jesus, that I was shocked to find out that some Christians actually drink beer. (I've since discovered that you can love Jesus and drink beer. Who knew?) Since those naïve days of my youth, I've been exposed to all the ugliness that we call humanity, inside and outside the church. When you follow Jesus, it comes with the territory. Or at least it should. When you pursue Him, He takes you closer and closer to people, and the closer you get to people (and the more honest you are with yourself), the more you realize there are some scary monsters hiding in our closets.

As the church, we tend to struggle with our monsters. We don't know how to deal with them, and we certainly don't know how to talk about them. We usually just push our dresser in front of the closet and pretend that we don't hear the growling coming from under the door. Then we smile as if we didn't even know monsters existed. We assume that just the mention of monsters will disqualify us, or worse, turn us into outcasts. Good news for us, some of God's most trusted servants assumed they were outcasts too.

In this chapter we'll talk about mercy, transparency, and hopefully we'll bust the myth that God only uses perfect people. We'll start by telling the story of the angry, stuttering, adopted son of an Egyptian princess.

BURIED IN THE SAND

If anyone in the Old Testament had monsters in his closet, it was Moses. Growing up apart from your parents in a foreign country has got to have a serious effect on you. No matter what he did, I assume he was always viewed as second best. He was forced to adopt the Egyptian way of doing things. He had to watch as his people were brutally enslaved. I wonder when he finally found out that he was a Hebrew, or did his Egyptian family always label him, "the Hebrew?" Either way, when we come across Moses' story in Exodus, we see a man who understands where he came from.

"...when Moses had grown up, he went out to visit his own people, the Hebrews, and he saw how hard they were forced to work. During his visit he saw an Egyptian beating one of his fellow Hebrews. After looking in all directions to make sure no one was watching, Moses killed the Egyptian and hid the body in the sand (Exodus 1:11-12)." Now, this seems like a bit of an overreaction. I've never been in Moses' situation, but premeditated murder isn't usually the best response to injustice. (Side note: If your pursuit of justice requires that you destroy people in the process of attaining it, you might want to rethink your strategy.)

Maybe pent up bitterness toward his Egyptian family had reached a boiling point, or maybe he just wanted to protect his people. No matter Moses' motives, there was still one dead Egyptian buried in the sand. So, out of fear for his own life, Moses fled Egypt to start over in Midian. All the while, he carried on his back the burden of his guilt and shame.

Years later, after Moses had married and become a shepherd, God came to him in a burning bush. Moses' response to God's request is classic. "O Lord, I'm not very good with words (Exodus 4:10)." I would have done the same thing, "Maybe if I talk about my speech impediment, God will forget that I'm a murderer." Apparently, it worked. God didn't even bring it up. Not a word about the dead Egyptian Moses buried in the sand.

Does this mean that God doesn't care about what we do? I don't think so. To me, it proves once again that God doesn't look at our list of accomplishments or our mound of transgressions. He looks at our hearts.

Moses gives us another great example of God's unexpected ways. He was qualified for leadership without lifting a finger, yet he wasn't disqualified from leadership despite his disgusting actions. You might be asking, "How can God stick with a murderer?" I get it, these stories usually illicit two types of reactions. One, anger. We can't understand how God could continue to use people who have done such horrible things. We believe they should be punished or at least removed from any sort of leadership role. The second reaction is relief. "If God can use Moses the murderer, then maybe He can use me."

If you are part of the group that thinks God isn't fair, be careful. This mindset usually springs from a faith that relies more on works than grace, and that's a scary place to live. There is something deadly that lives inside of us, and it is pride. Do whatever it takes to expel it from your heart.

If you are a part of the second group, I have good news. God isn't finished with you. He isn't frightened by what you've done. He can and will use you if you allow him to.

Despite his sin, Moses was considered "more humble than any other person on earth (Numbers 12:3)." How is that possible? I believe the key is how he viewed himself. This view allowed him to change into a meek and obedient servant. Moses knew that he was in need of repair but not beyond repair. He was keenly aware of his sin, yet He trusted God's judgment more than his own. (You need to read that last sentence over again.) So, even though Moses felt his sin had disqualified him, he still responded when God asked him to lead His people.

There is a fine line between allowing your past to humble you and allowing it to disqualify you. Use your past, let it remind you of where you came from, but don't let it dictate where you're going. Don't choose to drop out just because you think that at some point your past will catch up with you. Like thinking, "Eventually, they're going to figure out I'm not supposed to be here." God has you figured out – scars, spots and all – and He is still calling you.

I AM THE WORST OF THEM ALL

The first person I thought of when I was envisioning this chapter was Paul. If anyone could have pulled the "but you don't know what I've done" card, it was him. What must have been going through his mind when Jesus said, "Why are you persecuting me (Acts 9:4)?" That would have been the most frightening revelation. The whole time he had been convinced he was doing the will of the Father, when, in fact, he had been an adversary. Talk about a sinking feeling.

Maybe Paul was expecting a bolt of lightning to strike him dead where he stood. He probably deserved it. This was the same guy that "was uttering threats with every breath and was eager to kill the Lord's followers (Acts 9:1)." But instead of receiving the punishment he knew he deserved, he received an invitation. The unexplainable mercy of Jesus Christ met Paul on that road and offered him something unexpected – purpose.

Mercy is a difficult thing to grasp. I don't claim to understand it, but each year I have a better idea of what it isn't. It isn't fair, it isn't equitable, and it doesn't follow any sort of earthly guidelines. Mercy, in its purest form, can be infuriating. Especially if you secretly want people to get what they deserve. (Side note: If you ever want to do a heart check, just see how you react when someone who deserves to be punished gets rewarded.)

Our misunderstanding of mercy is one of the main reasons we disqualify ourselves because of our sin. We assume there is no way forward for us. There is only one way out of the prison cell we live in, and that is death. If we try really hard, we might be able to imagine the possibility of a pardon. "I guess He could let me off the hook." But never in our wildest dreams do we think God would not only remove our guilt but also use us to set other prisoners free. We can't comprehend it.

In his letter to Timothy, Paul writes, "I thank Christ Jesus our Lord, who has given me strength to do his work. He considered me trustworthy and appointed me to serve him, even though I used to blaspheme the name of Christ. In my insolence, I persecuted his people. But God had mercy on me… (1 Timothy 1:12-13)" We ask ourselves, "How can someone who blasphemed Jesus' name, hunted down Christians, and oversaw the stoning of Stephen be tasked with writing most of the New Testament and bringing the Gospel to the Gentile world? It makes no sense, weren't there holier people God could have chosen?"

I wonder how the early Church felt about Paul. Many of them would have known Stephen personally or at least admired his work with the widows of the community. They might even have been on the edge of the crowd as Stephen was stoned outside the walls of Jerusalem. I wonder if any of them would have remembered the young Pharisee holding the coats of the executioners and nodding with approval.

When Paul returned to Jerusalem with his testimony of meeting Jesus on the road to Damascus, the Church met him with fear rather than acceptance. It took the witness of Barnabas just to get Paul in the same room with the Apostles. I don't blame them, and I don't think Paul would have blamed them either. He later told Timothy, "Christ Jesus came into the world to save sinners – and I am the worst of them all (1 Timothy 1:15)." Paul fully understood who he was. He was an enemy of God. He had intimate knowledge of his own guilt. He knew the light of Jesus had mercifully cut through the fog of his sin. And, like Moses, he used the mistakes of his past as a tool to humble himself. His willingness to accept God's grace and mercy is what allowed him to write so eloquently on the very same subject throughout the New Testament.

I don't know if you have ever muttered the words, "But you don't know what I've done." My guess is, like me, you struggle daily with thoughts that remind you of how you've disqualified yourself. You think eventually "they" are going to find out how sinful you really are, and that will be that. It can feel like a prison. You end up spending your present thinking about your past rather than thinking about your future. You become stagnant, depressed, and visionless. Instead of dreaming, you mark off each day, one by one, on the wall of your jail cell.

Truthfully, the only person that can keep you in that prison is you. The cell door has already been opened. The guards are all gone. There are fresh clothes waiting on the table and plane tickets to wherever you want to go. God isn't standing in your way. What are you waiting for?

FILLED WITH LIGHT

"If you are filled with light, with no dark corners, then your whole life will be radiant, as though a floodlight were filling you with light (Luke 11:36)." On the road to Damascus, Saul (Paul) didn't have a choice whether to be filled with light or not. He got blasted by Jesus. Blinded. For the rest of us, the process isn't usually as dramatic.

There are plenty of days when I wish God would just circumvent my will and shine his spotlight into every little corner of my heart. I've come to the realization that the process usually requires a tad more effort on my part. I have to allow His light in.

But I find myself stuck between two mindsets. The first tells me that the people closest to me can't handle the truth. They won't look at me the same. They won't trust me anymore. The second is influenced by Scripture, "Confess your sins to each other and pray for each other so that you may be healed (James 5:16)." In order to move forward, to heal, to grow, I need to learn to be transparent. Directly correlated to the mindset I choose is the amount of light I allow Jesus to shine into my heart.

When we give into the lie that we have disqualified ourselves or that our crimes are unforgivable, we begin to close ourselves off from others. We only allow people in so far, not far enough to see the darkness inside of us. To me, that is the most destructive bi-product of hiding the monsters in our closets, the way it isolates us. Not just from God but from each other. We become islands, lonely and deserted, separated by miles of empty ocean. We actually fulfill our fear of being outcasts when we choose to keep our sins hidden. Instead of our friends and family sending us away, we send ourselves away.

The only way to overcome our policy of isolationism is to overcome our fears. I know, it's scary. Some of the most terrifying times in my life have been when I needed to confess something to a friend. Shaking, shortness of breath, heart palpitations. It's like jumping out of an airplane with someone, but they hold both parachutes. There is always that thought in the back of my mind, "They might just let me fall to my death."

But, just like overcoming any other fear, the rush when it's over is addicting. There are few things more satisfying than discovering that you're forgiven and accepted despite what you've done. It's like cheating death. Paul knew he deserved death, but what he got in return was life. My goal is to get you (and me, I need to do this too) to chase after transparency, to pursue a life lived out in the open. I want you to stop hiding the monsters in your closet and start to open up about them. When we hide our monsters, they grow and mutate and begin to control us. But when we expose them to the light, they shrivel and die.

A lifestyle of transparency has a profound effect on us, but it also has an unintended, life changing effect on the people around us. I've seen it happen time and again. A person will overcome their fear and open up about their "stuff." They fully expect faces of astonishment, but what they find are nods of agreement. They discover that almost everyone else struggles with the same thing. So transparency not only brings freedom to us, it brings freedom to others. When we stir up the courage to leave our prison cell, the other inmates realize their doors are unlocked too. It becomes a spiritual prison break.

One of the greatest gifts we can give someone is the understanding that what they've done or what they're going through isn't isolated only to them. Our transparency becomes a building block of relationship and community. When we are open about who we really are, we create the opportunity for deep connections with the people around us, for profound shared experiences. Our failures and mistakes, even though they seem so ugly and shameful to us, could be the key to freeing someone from their bonds of fear and shame.

Listen to me. I know it seems like you've done too much, but it doesn't matter what you've done. Give me a Bible and a few minutes, and I could find someone who has done something much worse than you. And God still used them to change the world. What matters is whether you're going to let Jesus redeem your past and give Him the freedom to dictate your future. It's time to pull back the curtains and let that afternoon sunshine spill in.

Even now, as you finish this chapter, begin to talk to God about the sins that have held you back. Talk to Him about the sins that have kept you on the sidelines, the sins that have caused you to label yourself a second class Christian. Take your guilt and shame and exchange it for the truth of how He sees you. You are not disqualified.

6

It Costs Too Much

I'm not going to argue with you on this one. It does cost a lot. Following your dreams, starting something – these are expensive propositions. When my wife and I decided to leave our quaint little North Idaho town and move to South Africa, I never imagined how many things we would have to give up. Relocating to the other side of the world sounds so exciting until you get the bill.

First of all, we had to get rid of everything. It starts off pretty fun, especially as an American, because you have so much crap. It's no big deal giving away a couple of T-shirts when you have another forty in the closet. (I think, at one point, we gave away thirty garbage bags full of clothes...what?!) But after awhile, when your daughter is deciding which stuffed animal she wants to take with her, it starts to wear on you.

Secondly, you have to give up all of your other possible paths. We could have stayed in Idaho, continued to pastor at the church we'd been at for sixteen years, lived next door to our kids' school, all the while creating cute traditions that we would pass on to our grandchildren. That was an option. What I had failed to understand up to that point in my life was, in order to chase a dream or a calling, sometimes you have to let go of another dream. Sure, there are times God backs you into a corner and there's only one way forward, but plenty of other times there are two or three equally awesome paths, and you just have to choose one.

My wife would tell you that she wasn't super stoked to trade the American dream for the African safari. She wasn't overjoyed when her dream house was being emptied of all of our things, and the relative stability that she had enjoyed was evaporating before her eyes. I'm not sure either of us had fully calculated the cost of our decision.

Thirdly, it can cost you your family and friends. Yes, you heard that right. Almost all of our family and friends were within a three hour drive of us, and then we went and replaced that three hour drive with a nine hour flight, followed by an eleven hour flight, followed by a one hour flight, followed by a forty five minute drive (approximately 10,000 total miles). No more winter journeys to grandma's house for Christmas. No more play dates with the kids down the street. No more dreams of Kindle and True growing up with their cousins. We traded it all in to start something new.

Now that I've got all of the depressing stuff out of the way, let's talk about the price of adventure. Is it worth it? Let's find out.

If there is one area where I lack spiritual muscles, it's in the area of finances. I can have faith for a lot of crazy things, but if there is a big dollar figure attached to it, I freeze up. I haven't quite figured out why that is. Maybe it's because I didn't have a lot of money growing up. Maybe, somewhere deep inside of me, I think money equals security. I'm not sure, but all I know is it's a struggle. So when we crunched the numbers for our adventurous journey to Cape Town, my blood pressure might have spiked.

The sentence, "It costs too much," probably bounced around in my head as I pondered the feasibility of our plan. The faith-filled side of my brain was like, "It'll be fine!" while the less than certain side of me was wondering if maybe I could sell a kidney. That is usually my first reaction to any sort of financial challenge. What can I do to make it happen? The problem with this line of thinking is that when a dream with a seemingly insurmountable price tag takes shape in your mind, you spend all your time coming up with reasons why it won't work. My challenge was to either stretch my faith or choose a more palatable dream to pursue.

I'm sure this whole process makes God laugh. He goes to great lengths in the Bible to remind us that He will take care of our needs. "Seek the Kingdom of God above all else, and live righteously, and he will give you everything you need (Matthew 6:33)." Even though He promises to take care of us, we let a little thing like money stop us. Do we really think the God who created ten trillion galaxies, each with one hundred billion stars (by the way, that's probably a gross underestimation), is going to break a sweat taking care of our bank accounts? The fact that God can put a dream in our frail little hearts that has the capacity to grow into a world changing destiny is more amazing to me than the fact He can pay for it all.

It's just money. I'm not saying you should sell everything you own and move to the other side of the world (unless God is telling you to do that, then by all means). What I am saying is money should never be the reason you stay home. As my good friend Pastor David Warnick would say, "It's the cost of doing business." Pursuing your destiny will cost you something. It will take some risk on your part.

Over the last couple of years I have tried to reinvent myself as a spiritual entrepreneur. What is that, you say? I know, it sounds pretty cool. Basically, I have tried to change how I look at the finances I have been given. I have always been a decent steward, but my type of stewardship was more about protecting what I had in preparation for disaster, instead of investing what I had in preparation for a brighter future. I had never thought of investing money in the Kingdom because that was for rich people, right?

Becoming a spiritual entrepreneur is about looking for opportunities to take risks and investing in what God is doing in the world. It's about giving your time, energy, talents, and money (yes, money) to something that stirs your heart and your passion.

I'll give you an example. Last year, I got a burden on my heart for Germany. I don't know why. I had just moved to Cape Town, and I thought that was burden enough. My sister (Caiti) lives in Munich, so there was a bit of a connection. In the past, when I felt something similar, I would start praying for God to provide, and then wait until that provision materialized.

This time was different. I felt like God was saying, "What are you waiting for? I already paid for this."

"Wait, God, you want me to use our savings to invest in Germany?"

The idea that God had prepaid for the desires of my heart had never crossed my mind. The money wasn't coming; it was already there in my bank account. The thought was at once both freeing and petrifying. It meant I had to invest what God had already put in my hands. I couldn't keep it to better secure my future; I needed to use it in the hope that it would better secure someone else's future. What this taught me was that to become a spiritual entrepreneur, I had to risk not just my life and my reputation but my financial security as well.

Does that make it any easier? No, absolutely not. I am naturally risk averse, cautious. Just last night I had a deep conversation with Aimee about how I think about finances, and let's just say it wasn't pretty. Every time I feel like I have some thought traction, I slide back into old ways of thinking, and my wife has to dig me out. She's good at that.

If this seems too much to handle, then we're in the same boat. This stuff is hard and scary. For many of us it's uncharted waters, but we can't ignore the truth resting at the core of these great challenges. The truth that God is calling us out of our comfort zone and into His grand adventure. That truth confronts our perfectly constructed sensibilities, and we're presented with a choice. We either pursue that truth into the unknown, putting ourselves in one uncomfortable and faith stretching position after another. Or we retreat into the relative "safety" of life as we know it.

When is a dream too costly? At what price do you walk away saying, "I could never afford that?" At what point does the sticker shock drive you back to the section of the dream store that is, "more in my price range?" What would it be like to get to the point where when Jesus drops a crazy dream in our hearts, we don't even look at the price tag? We just buy it. Whatever the cost. Because, to us, it is worth every penny.

SAFETY FIRST

If you haven't figured it out yet, I'm your number one fan. OK, maybe not number one, but I'm probably third behind your Mom and Grandma. I want you to try impossible things. I want you to climb Mount Everest, walk on the moon, and break the sound barrier. But all of those things are pretty dangerous. If you want to stay safe, then we are getting to the point where you might want to put the book down. It only gets more dangerous from here.

Did anyone ever tell you that following Jesus was the safest option? Eternally it is, but while you're still on the earth? I'm sorry if you've been under the impression that responding to the call of Jesus meant you would stay comfortable. Jesus made it pretty clear when He said, "I am sending you out as sheep among wolves (Matthew 10:16)." That sounds fairly uncomfortable. Does Jesus know what wolves do to sheep?

If I'm being honest, my initial response to the wolf news would be to build a wolf proof fence with wolf motion sensors and hire around the clock wolf security. You can never be too careful. But the problem with fences is that you are only safe when you hide behind them. Even then, there's always the chance that one of the sheep behind the fence with you is not what he or she claims to be.

God said, "I am sending you out..." We tend to skip over that part of the verse. When we hear the word "wolves," we start building our bunkers and try to hold out until heaven. But did God warn us of wolves so we could spend our lives digging holes and hiding? I hope not. It sounds horribly claustrophobic.

You might be saying, "Mat, I want to make sure I'm hearing you right. Are you saying that, even though there are wolves out beyond our fences, we should still go out there? That seems foolish." Yes, that is what I am saying, and it does seem foolish. But I'll go one further and say that, as long as you are holding the hand of fear, wherever he leads you will not be safe. Even if it's a wolf proof bunker.

I have come to realize that all of my own fences and bunkers are only a pathetic attempt to control my life, to control the chaos and unpredictability surrounding me. I set up electric fences in an attempt to control my "neighbors" (or at least prevent their dogs from pooping on my lawn), but how much control do I really have over my "neighbors?" How much control do I have over anything?

I can't control the weather, the traffic, the economy. No matter how hard I try, I can't prevent my daughter from breaking her arm at school (or the cost of medical bills that will follow). Oh but I try, and it's exhausting! Nothing in my life drains me faster than striving to control that which is impossible to control. Just this week I about drove myself mad trying to control the South African visa renewal process. As if the key to unlocking the South African bureaucracy was my personal anxiety levels.

Why do I do it? The only thing I can control is myself, but I spend all my energy trying to control everything else. This turns me into a grumpy, short-tempered brat who takes out his frustration on the people he loves the most. My inability to control the South African government led to tension between me, my wife, and my daughter. Seriously?! It sounds so stupid when I write it, but it's real. In an effort to gain control of my surroundings, I lost control of me.

Hopefully, you can relate to what I'm saying. It would be so awkward if I'm the only one struggling with this. What are you trying to control? What bunkers have you built to keep yourself safe? How effective have your "neighbor" proof fences been? How do you react to uncontrollable circumstances in your life?

So much of this life is out of our hands. Honestly, that's a good thing. (I've seen how you drive, Jesus take the wheel!) Maybe it's time to let go. So what if life is unpredictable and unsafe. Let's embrace it! Embrace the chaos, enjoy the ride, stop wasting your time trying to control what can't be controlled. Spend your time trying to control the only thing God gave you the liberty to control – yourself. (Side note: if that sounded intense it's because I am kind of yelling those words at myself...loudly)

I have a picture in my mind of Jesus walking through the middle of a tornado with a smile on His face. Dirt and debris swirling violently around Him, but He is just strolling along like He's got no place to go. I think the disciples saw that same Jesus asleep in the boat as the storm raged around them. That Jesus, the one that we assume is oblivious to the danger, is looking at us like we're the crazy ones as we scream, "Are you just going to stand there while the world falls apart?!" That Jesus is calling through the chaos of our lives and asking, "Do you trust me?"

We can try with all our might but the wolves and the tornados will find us, even behind the steel doors of our bunkers. What will we do then? Will we nearly kill ourselves with stress and anxiety by trying to control the uncontrollable, or will we give up control, in the midst of the chaos, to the only One who can calm the storm outside and inside of us? It's time to stop listening to the voice that's saying, "Play it safe," and start listening to the voice that's saying, "You're safe with me."

DECISION MAKING PARALYSIS

All our penny pinching and safety regulations hinder our ability to make decisions. The only decisions we end up making are the ones that happen to fall within our price and comfort range. Even then, we struggle to choose because we can't completely control the outcome. The inability to guarantee the results of our decisions begins this process of paralysis.

Let me give you a recent example. A couple weeks back I was forced into buying a car. I say "forced" because I would never willingly enter into that process. I already struggle with making big purchases, but then force me to make that frightening financial decision in a foreign country and I become a ticking stress bomb. That stress and anxiety led to weeks of second guessing. I would do my research and "confidently" make a decision one moment, and then thirty minutes later completely change my mind. "Is it really the right car? Is it too small? Does it have good enough fuel economy? Is it a fair price? Is it reliable? Is it too old? What if it turns out to be a lemon?" I could type a few more paragraphs, but I'll save you the trouble.

I was paralyzed. I needed to move forward, but I couldn't. It had such an effect on my thinking that I didn't write a single word in this book for almost two weeks. It was like I fell into a mud pit. In my pursuit of the perfect decision, I had created a scenario where a decision was impossible.

When I analyze my own thought processes, and the countless conversations I have had with people over the years, I find there a couple different reasons why we struggle so much to decide.

One, we think there is always a "right" and "wrong" to every choice. For instance, let's say you are choosing which university to attend. You have a choice between four schools that have accepted your application. We assume that three of the universities are the "wrong" choice and one is "right." We pull our hair out over decisions like these. "What if I make the 'wrong' choice and miss God's plan for my life?"

Do we really think God's plan for our life is so fragile and delicate that all it takes is one of our choices to ruin the whole thing? I believe that if your heart really wants what God wants, then there can be multiple "right" answers. If your love for God is at the forefront of your mind then you could choose any of the four universities, and it wouldn't destroy His plans for you. (Side note: I think God is more concerned with the amount of worry and fear that we attach to our decisions than He is with which university we choose.) I always tell people that if a choice you are about to make is really going to have adverse effects on the plan of God for your life, He will let you know. If He sent His only son to die for you, then we can assume He is highly invested in your future.

Two, we are control freaks. I spoke a little about this earlier, and it should be repeated. We struggle to make decisions because we can't control the outcome. Part of our problem is that we judge our decisions based on how they turn out. For instance, if the car I chose to purchase breaks down or has problems, then in hindsight I made a poor decision. This thinking leads us to believe there is some magical, problem free path awaiting us if we make all the right decisions. If we experience something negative or painful then we must have made a bad decision along the way.

The myth of this magical, problem free path puts extra pressure on every decision, and that extra pressure causes most of us to forfeit our right to choose. We realize we can't control the outcome, so we find it preferable to just not choose at all.

I've found that my lack of choosing causes me as much pain as my choices. The strain, stress, and worry I go through trying to make the perfect decision is far worse than the discomfort of dealing with the outcome. Maybe you've felt the same thing, the pressure of trying to be perfect. It's painful, I know, but it doesn't have to be this way. You and I can stop trying to control everything, and choose to believe that God has our backs. If we can choose to believe that, the other choices get easier.

I'm convinced that life is more about Who you choose and less about what you choose. (Take a second to let that last sentence sink in.) If you're concerned about the desires of His heart and His will, then be free of your decision making paralysis. Make a choice, even if it costs you something. God knows all about decisions like that.

Part 3

Why We Should

7

Life is Short

As I write this sentence, I am three months from my thirty seventh birthday. (That doesn't sound right.) Either you will say, "Wow, he is old!" or "He's just a baby." To me, it's old enough. People tell you that time flies, that you should stop and smell the roses. They're right. Life is short. I blinked and my high school graduation is turning into my twenty year reunion. How is that possible? Last week I was helping someone fill out a university application, and when they entered their birth year I almost choked. There is no way a high school senior was born in 1998.

Needless to say, we have limited time on this earth. None of us know the day when death will come knocking on our door, and no one can respond to that knock but us. What are we going to do with the time that we have left? It could be ten weeks, ten months, or ten years. How do you want to spend it?

I purposefully chose the word spend because time is a commodity just like money, but unlike money we don't know how much of it we have. We only know of the little we hold in our hand at this moment, the present. How are we going to spend the present? Some of us spend it in the past, either dreaming of the good old days or regretting mistakes. Some of us spend it in the future, dreaming we'll magically win the lottery or at least hoping things will be different. But the only way the future can be affected is by the choices we make now, in this moment.

My hope is that while you read this chapter you will realize the power you have right now and the myriad possibilities lying before you. Sure, you could wait to start something until after high school...college...after you're married...after the kids have left the house...after you've retired. Or you could start now. The choice is yours.

WHAT TO DO WITH WHAT'S LEFT

I have a "fun" little exercise I have done with our interns over the years. It involves estimating the time we have and how we use it. (I'm not doing this to depress you. Hopefully, it will have the opposite effect. Should we give it a go? Ok! Let's start by giving ourselves something generous like a ninety year lifespan. That is better than average (the average lifespan of an American is somewhere around seventy eight years), and I think we'd all be happy with living longer than the average person.

First, let's take a look at the necessities – sleeping, eating, etc. We'll subtract the time we sleep from the ninety years we've been given. I just chose eight hours of sleep arbitrarily, some will sleep more and some will sleep less, but it seems like a good place to start. So if we sleep eight hours per night for ninety years, by the time we die we will have slept for one third of our life (almost 263,000 hours). Thirty years! Let that sink in.

Let's move on to eating. Let's be generous again and say that our food preparation and consumption only takes two hours of our day. Most days it's much more than that, especially if you are cooking at home, but two will have to do. By the time we die, we'll have spent 7.5 years cooking and eating food. (I'm not even factoring in grocery shopping.)

Ok, what about hygiene? Hopefully, we see this as a necessity. Maybe in junior high we didn't, but those days are long gone. Right? Showering, brushing our teeth, flossing (I must confess I usually skip this one...apologies to my dentist), going number one and number two, etc. Again, I think I'm being generous (especially considering how long my brother, Caleb, spends in the bathroom), but let's go with a solid hour. That works out to 3.75 years in the bathroom, and probably a high percentage of those years are spent on the toilet. We now have 48.75 years left.

But let's be honest. How much can we really do when we are kids? We have very little control over our lives until we're at least teenagers. Some of us don't feel independent until we're eighteen, but we also know kids who started making an impact well before their eighteenth birthdays. How about we choose fifteen as a cutoff point? Let's say that before fifteen it's more about our parents' decisions than our own. So, after we subtract our formative years, we're left with 33.75 years out of our ninety. This is starting to get scary.

OK, what about leisure activities, such as watching TV? The average American watches about five hours of TV per day, but we aren't average, are we? We are way better. But let's also throw in Netflix, Facebook, Twitter, Pinterest, Instagram, etc. When you factor in the time we normally spend on all of it, I would have to guess that at least four hours of our normal day is spent engaged in some form of media. Let's be real, it's bad. Four hours of daily media interaction works out to fifteen years of our lives spent looking at TV's, computer screens, or smartphones. We are now left with 18.75 years of our ninety.

I haven't even factored in the years we spend driving from point A to point B, exercising, putting our kids to bed, or writing twelve page papers for some random English class we didn't want to take in the first place. I could go on, but I think we all get the point. The clock is ticking.

For me, it's been ticking for awhile now already. If I live until I'm ninety then I've only got 53ish years left, minus 17ish years of sleeping, minus 4ish years of eating, minus 2ish years in the bathroom. That gives me thirty years to do everything else, and if I end up binge watching a few series on Netflix (which I have been known to do) then that thirty becomes ten (maybe I'm exaggerating a bit). What am I going to do with that time? Will I finally learn German or write another book, visit New Zealand or watch Liverpool play at Anfield? Will I laugh with my kids, dance with my wife, forgive the ones who have hurt me, love the unlovable? Or will I let my days pass from one to the next until I'm left with nothing but a handful of wishes?

What will you do with the time you have left? There is one key word in that question...DO. Not what do you wish would happen in the time you have left, but what are you actually going to do?! Good intentions are wonderful, but good intentions quickly transform into regrets without action. Action is the key. And if your actions come from an obedient, God-centered heart, they can have eternal ramifications. When the thing that's in your heart is transmitted to your hands and feet, you have the ability to make an impact that transcends time, an impact that can change someone else's eternity.

What am I trying to say? Just start moving forward. It might not seem like it, but there are people out there who need you to start moving. God will guide your steps, but only you can take those steps. Only an act of your will can move you out of the starting blocks. The clock is ticking. It's your move.

A MORNING FOG

So, I just spent the last few paragraphs acting like we're all going to live until we're ninety (wouldn't that be awesome?), and maybe you've known a few grandparents who have made it to that golden age (my Grandma Polly comes to mind). But the truth is we have no idea how long we're going to live. As I was driving this morning, someone swerved into my lane, and if I hadn't been paying attention (Side note: Stop looking at your phone while you drive! Seriously, stop!), I probably would have hit that SUV head on. All of my fancy plans for the future would have come to an end at the ripe old age of thirty six, and this book would have had four less chapters.

Even though most of us have had similar close calls in our lives, we still live like we're invincible, like nothing can stop us. I'm as guilty as anyone. I say things like, "I'll get to that when I have more time," but I'm never going to have more time. From the moment the doctor spanked my butt in the delivery room, my countdown clock started. No matter how hard I try, I can't add a second to that clock. The only power I have is in how I spend those seconds.

James writes, "How do you know what your life will be like tomorrow? Your life is like the morning fog--it's here a little while, then it's gone (James 4:14)." James compares the span of our lives to a cloud of tiny water droplets that arrives before dawn but is burned away by lunch time. Depressing. Thanks, James. But he's right. We don't know what tomorrow will bring or if we'll even make it to tomorrow. We have to take full advantage of today.

A couple weeks ago, I found out that my Grandma Jeanie – the most graceful and faith-filled woman you will ever meet – was given six months to live by her doctors. I took the news the way most people would probably take it, hard. Her house was less than a mile from the house I grew up in, so I used to show up at her doorstep randomly for various baked goodies. She was the perfect combination of gentle and firm, which I'm sure she learned from raising six boys. Whenever she finally goes home to be with the Lord, I am going to miss her so much.

I bring up her story because when I heard about her diagnosis it made me think about how I would react if I were in her position. If a doctor told me, "Mr. Thomason, I'm sorry to tell you this, but you have six months to live." What things would I immediately stop caring about? How many things that I'm worried about today would I cease to worry about tomorrow? (I'm positive Seahawks' losses wouldn't affect me as much as they do right now.) What would be left on my priority list? Who would I want to see, to speak with, to laugh with? My hope is that I would make everyone's lives around me better. I would want to inject as much joy as possible into every day and would make sure people know what a privilege it is to be alive.

People like to use the phrase "live like you are dying" in order to motivate people, and it works sometimes. You hear it in songs, read it on posters, but it's hard to find anyone who is actually living as if they are dying. It usually takes a tragedy to do that. How sad is it that we need a tragedy to remind us to make each day count?

I think the phrase needs to be tweaked a little to add emphasis. "Live because you're dying." The more I think about it, the more I want to tattoo it on my forehead so I see it every time I look in the mirror. (I wouldn't actually get a tattoo. I'm still afraid of my Mom.) What am I doing with the decades – or years – or months – or days – that I have left? If I'm dying, am I living? Am I taking it all in, cataloging each moment as it passes? Am I investing in eternal things? Am I present in each moment with my wife, my kids, and my friends? Am I allowing my passion to have an impact each day, or are my days just passing me by?

What about you? If Saint James is right, then the morning fog of our life is being burned away as we speak. What are you going to do? There has never been a better time than the present to start something. Why don't you decide right now that tomorrow is going to be the best tomorrow you've ever had? Not because of what tomorrow will bring, but because of what you'll bring to tomorrow. Wake up early, watch the sunrise, and start to look at every moment like an opportunity, because life is short.

8

There is Only One of You

You can look at the phrase "there is only one of you" from a couple different angles. From one perspective it sounds like a taunt, something a bully would say to his prey. "You and what army?" A perfectly crafted series of words meant to strike fear in the heart of its victim. Sounds like a good excuse to back down, especially if you are faced with the decision of either giving up your lunch money or getting punched in the face.

We've all been there. Our passion for some worthy cause is stoked to the point of action when suddenly the "wisdom and logic" of our mind reminds us how foolish the task before us is. "There is only one of you." As if we didn't already feel small enough, these words are always there to make sure we never forget our place. "What can one person do?"

But what if we changed the camera angle just a bit and looked at these words from a different perspective? There is no one else in the world like you. You are the one and only you. Instead of making you feel like a dwarf in a room full of giants, these words should challenge you to be everything you were meant to be, because no one can be you but you. (I just said "you" five times in that sentence.)

If all goes to plan, the next time a bully singles you out on the playground and taunts you with the words, "There is only one of you," you'll be able to respond with, "Yeah, what's your point?"

This chapter is about understanding how important we are, not just as a placeholder until someone better comes along, but as an integral part of the plans and purposes of God. Each one of us is special, unique, and meant for something great. We'll talk about how unique you are (Don't get carried away, I'm unique too.) and the importance of pursuing your dreams.

But first, let's start by working on a puzzle together.

THE MISSING PUZZLE PIECE

Aimee and I used to lead a Friday night small group at our house. It was mostly made up of young adults whom we had known for years, former/current interns, and the occasional random person. (Don't worry, they didn't stay random for long.) Our nights were usually made up of worship, food, and some sort of group discussion. I say usually because there were other times where we would do things out of the ordinary.

Like this one time, someone (I can't remember who) brought up the idea of working on a puzzle together. Immediately, I was like, "Uh, what?!" But my wife is the most positive, inclusive, and caring person in the world, so she was like, "Yay! That sounds fun!" So, of course, Aimee won.

I can't recall how many pieces it was, but it felt like 175,000. The picture was of a series of ice cream cones Photoshopped on top of one another. I wish I could explain it better than that, but I can't. It was super trippy to look at, which made it extremely difficult to complete. We had more than a few nights of frustration.

It took us weeks and weeks to finish the puzzle. Somehow we kept it on our dining room table the entire time without one of our kids completely destroying it. A minor miracle. One of the coolest things about the process of completing it was that the team that worked on it each week was different (except for Aimee and I because it was at our house). Young adults aren't always the most consistent people in the world (no offense, guys), which left us with a rotating starting lineup of jigsaw junkies. It was interesting how each person saw the puzzle just a little bit differently than the other people at the table and what section each person chose to work on.

Fast forward to the last Friday night of our epic quest. It must have been at least a couple of months leading up to this point. We only had maybe fifty puzzle pieces left. There was a moment, frozen in time, where we thought we were missing a piece. I wish I could put into words the terror and anguish that descended on our home at that moment. Let's just say there was talk off lighting things on fire. We searched for that piece for what seemed like decades; under the couch cushions, under the table, in our pockets, in our shoes. We stopped just short of tearing up the laminate flooring. Right before we collectively lost our minds, the final piece emerged from its hiding place (probably somewhere we had already looked). We all took a deep breath and whispered a barely audible, "Hallelujah." Crisis averted.

Remember, there were approximately 175,000 pieces that made up this puzzle, and we almost rioted over one missing piece. You're like, "Of course you nearly stormed the streets, turned over parked cars, and looted storefronts, there is nothing more unjust in the history of mankind than finding out you are missing one puzzle piece!" I agree with you, 100%. No matter how many pieces a puzzle has, you need every piece in order to complete the picture.

Now, imagine a puzzle with seven billion pieces, each one unique. You would think with a puzzle of that size each piece would have less importance than if you were working on a puzzle with, say, one hundred pieces. But anyone who has ever failed to put together a huge puzzle because of one missing piece knows that the greater the puzzle, the greater the worth of each piece.

And now we come to you, piece number 1,443,583,277. (I'm just guessing at your number, I could be off by a couple digits.) You've got a little blue in one of your corners, but you're mostly greens and browns. Maybe you're not a huge fan of earth tones. Maybe you've looked in the mirror and said, "I can't be that important. I'm sure they won't miss me. They can just find someone else to take my place." So you sit on your couch (a couch made for puzzle pieces), watching TV, waiting for the day when the puzzle is completed and you finally get to see what it looks like.

Just so you know, you're going to be waiting on that couch for a very long time. You were wrong. We can't find anyone to take your place. We've tried shoving other pieces into your spot, and it just doesn't work. We need you in all of your earth toned brilliance, and until we get you we are going to be at least one piece short.

Did you know that starting something so small, like believing there is a place for you, would also mean finishing something so huge? I didn't either. We're all so connected to each other. Our actions have ripple effects in the world around us. Even our failure to act has far reaching consequences. We might never see it, but it's still true. We think we are helping by excluding ourselves, but we are actually preventing the completion of the very thing we dream of most.

You can't sit this one out. God has created such a beautiful picture and put specific pieces in each of our hearts. It is going to take all of us, being who He made us to be, to complete it.

THE WORLD NEEDS YOUR DREAM

Dreaming is like breathing; it's a natural thing. It just happens. No one needs to teach us to dream, but sometime between pretending to be superheroes and our first utility bill, we stop. We trade our old sports car of an imagination in for the new minivan of practicality (There is nothing wrong with owning a minivan; it's just an analogy.), because at some point we have to grow up.

We were all asked the question when we were kids, "What do you want to be when you grow up?" The answer is usually something like firefighter, princess, police officer, doctor, ballerina, or astronaut. Epic stuff. And adults are always so encouraging when you're a kid. You never hear an adult say to a five year old, "Really? Astronaut? Maybe you should pursue a more practical profession." The response is usually, "That's great! You can grow up to be whatever you want to be, Billy!"

At some point the advice changes from, "Shoot for the stars," to "Don't quit your day job." It's no wonder most people hate what they do. They aren't doing what they imagined when they were a kid. They aren't pursuing artistic, heroic, world changing things. They're just settling for a life that someone else manufactured for them in a factory.

When we were kids, we didn't care whether or not our dreams came with steady paychecks. In our little naïve" minds, saving lives, exploring new frontiers, and creating beautiful things were the only payments we required. It was never about planning for retirement or climbing the corporate ladder. It was about doing something that made even the tiniest cells inside of us tingle with delight. Maybe fear got in the way. Or money. Or both. Whatever it was that changed us, it isn't too late.

The world needs us to stop growing up and to start dreaming again. Unlock the closet in the back of your mind where your imagination is kept, and let it stretch its legs. It didn't die when you became an adult. It's been waiting impatiently for you. Let it run. Imagine impossible things, things that would make "grown ups" chuckle, things that would require miracles. Then never stop – no matter what they say – don't stop dreaming.

Have I gotten you sufficiently fired up? OK. Now remember, the title of this section is "The World Needs Your Dream." But just because it's your dream doesn't mean it's only for you. Our dreams can start with us, but it's tragic if they end with us. To make more sense of what I mean, let's examine the dream of a daddy's boy named Joseph.

"One night Joseph had a dream, and when he told his brothers about it, they hated him more than ever. 'Listen to this dream,' he said. 'We were out in the field, tying up bundles of grain. Suddenly my bundle stood up, and your bundles all gathered around and bowed low before mine!' His brothers responded, 'So you think you will be our king, do you? Do you actually think you will reign over us?' And they hated him all the more because of his dreams and the way he talked about them (Genesis 37:5-8)."

So in Joseph's dream, he is ruling over his brothers even though he's the youngest and probably weakest of the crew. At seventeen I can only imagine what I would have been thinking. "Alright, God must have realized how much better I am than my brothers. He just wanted to reassure me that, at some point, they will recognize my leadership genius as well."

We don't know for certain the tone Joseph used to tell his brothers about his dream, but based on their reaction, he might have come across a little cocky. It even says in the passage that, "they hated him because...of the way he talked about [his dreams]." I think, based on that evidence, Joseph thought his dream was all about him. He couldn't have imagined the part he would eventually play, because he was only able to see his dream from a limited, self-centered point of view.

Fast forward roughly twenty years. We see the same brothers who sold Joseph into slavery now standing before him starving. After thirteen years in slavery and prison, and nine years as overseer of Egypt, the vision he saw as a seventeen year old was taking shape right before his eyes. His brothers – on their knees – begging for mercy. He stood with the authority to do anything he wished. He must've rehearsed this moment a hundred times while he was in prison, but something inside of him had changed.

Instead of responding with, "Ha ha ha, I told you idiots you were going to bow down to me, and here you are! How does it feel, suckers?!" Joseph said, "God has sent me ahead of you to keep you and your families alive... (Genesis 45:7)" He had discovered that his self-centered, teenage dream wasn't really about him. The dream that God put in his heart wasn't about his position of authority and the subjugation of his brothers, it was about their salvation.

Now, back to you. Yes, the world needs your dream. But the reason it needs it isn't because it needs another celebrity to worship or a ruler to exalt. We already have enough of those. No, the world needs your dream because any dream that comes from God has one purpose, and that purpose is to save lives. He made you unique and gave you unique dreams to save many lives. The sooner you realize that, the better it will be for all of us.

9

Love

I had a mini-revelation yesterday (is there such a thing as a mini-revelation?) as I was sitting on an airplane, pondering life. I thought, "I don't love my wife well enough, and I can be a selfish jerk sometimes." (I'm sure Aimee would totally disagree with the first part of that statement, but maybe not the second part.) I've probably thought that hundreds of times over our twelve years of marriage, but this time it stuck in my brain. It stuck in such a way that I decided to do something about it (Isn't it nice when we actually decide to respond to conviction?). I started processing the different ways that I had fallen short in my love for Aimee. Then I just started thinking of ways that I could put my love in action because love without action is...well, it's not love at all.

Right in the middle of that journey from revelation to activation another thought entered my mind. "If I can't even love Aimee well, how will I ever be able to love anyone else the way they should be loved?" (Don't get depressed. I was just having a moment. I know that it is possible to love people well.)

Then the faces of all of my family, friends, acquaintances, random people I walk by at the store, the people sitting beside me on the airplane, and the drivers I clog the roads with on Mondays started to flash through my mind. I realized that I had the time and capability to love all of these people well, but I had let my agenda and personal priorities stand in the way of loving them the way they should be loved. My personal (and slightly selfish) agenda had created an atmosphere of frustration, competitiveness, and stress.

Most of us live our entire lives in that atmosphere. If you watch the news or follow your Twitter feed for more than thirty minutes you'll realize that the atmosphere we've created is having an adverse effect on our world. It looks and feels like hate is winning. We live in a world that is operating out of a love deficit. That deficit has created a society at war with itself. A society that is underloved, one that will claw and fight for every scrap of affection, attention, and validation that it can sink its teeth into. Because of that love deficit our default language has become sarcasm. (I'm probably the guiltiest of all. I find it easier to be sarcastic than encouraging. I'm working on it.) We've become experts at tearing each other apart, but we struggle to protect even the weakest among us. Maybe the only way to begin to shift the love deficit to a love surplus is to stop trying to protect ourselves.

In this chapter we'll talk about the unavoidable pain of love and the power of forgiveness. Hopefully, by the end, we'll be left with only one course of action...love.

One of the biggest reasons we hold back our love from the world is our inability to embrace the pain of love. We all know love is painful; we've been burned one too many times. And because of our intimate knowledge of that pain, we create structures that buffer us from it. Our goal is to create a pain free existence, but we end up creating a love free existence instead.

We're always looking for the sure bet. We want to know that the object of our love will never break our heart, that they'll never leave us, which creates a fear of commitment. That fear, along with others, has changed our definition of love. Love has become more about good feelings and affection, and when those good feelings change, we "fall out of love." What if we embraced a different definition of love, one that included vulnerability and sacrifice?

"Great idea, Mat! Why don't you just ask me to walk into oncoming traffic? Are you trying to get me killed?"

Well, kind of. I believe that love and pain go hand in hand, and we can't love the way Jesus loved until we die to ourselves. So, yeah, I am trying to get you killed. Sorry (but I'm not really sorry). If you want to really love, you need to embrace not only the painful possibility of broken trust and betrayal but also the pain of personal sacrifice. Jesus endured both for us.

When we think of the cost of Jesus' love, the crucifixion immediately comes to mind. The extreme physical pain that He went through for our sake. His sacrifice. When we are feeling brave we say things like, "I will take up my cross and follow Him." We focus on the physical pain of the cross for the sake of the Gospel, but when it's time for the relational crucifixion we find ourselves making excuses. "I'm sure Jesus wants me to live a pain free life, right?"

Don't forget, Jesus' love forced him to endure more than just physical agony. He also endured a broken heart for us. He was betrayed, sold out for thirty pieces of silver, by one of his closest friends. Another one of His friends denied that he even knew Him on three separate occasions, "He was despised and rejected-- a man of sorrows, acquainted with deepest grief. We turned our backs on him and looked the other way. He was despised, and we did not care (Isaiah 53:3)."

Jesus knew how painful His choice to love us would be, yet He still endured it all for us. I believe that in order for us to fully understand who we are in the light of who He is, then we have to embrace the pain of love. We can't hide behind our walls of hurt and offense anymore. We can't wait around for the "sure thing" that we are convinced will never break our heart. Jesus became the "sure thing" for us, so we have no need to fear what might happen to us if we love the way He did.

If we want to follow in Jesus' loving footsteps then we can't be surprised or shrink back when He leads us into painful territory. I understand that we just met nine chapters ago, but trust me when I say that I have full confidence in your ability to follow Jesus anywhere, even there. Even to that self-sacrificing place of love we reserve only for the saints. But it's going to take an act of your will to make it happen.

Love is a choice, and sometimes choices have painful consequences. As long you put pain in the "bad" category, those consequences will always seem negative. (Side note: Along with pain comes growth and healing. When we run from pain, we run from discipleship and restoration.) In order to embrace the pain, we need to allow ourselves to see the benefits of pain. To see pain as a means to a beautiful end, to see it as a path to strength and depth in relationships.

If we want to shrink the love deficit, then we need to embrace the pain that comes from sacrificing ourselves for others and choose to love at a level where our heart is fully engaged and vulnerable. Jesus already modeled it for us. All we need to do is follow His lead.

FORGIVE AND FORGET

I want to return to the story of Joseph, the teenage dreamer, one more time. I'm sure you can recall his journey from son to slave to prisoner to ruler. The amount of personal pain he endured is staggering. Most of us will never experience that level of betrayal in our lifetimes. If anyone would have had a free pass to hate, it was Joseph.

Any normal person would have been plotting revenge, praying for the moment when they could pay their brothers back evil for evil. But something happened to Joseph between the day he was sold by his brothers, and the day they returned seeking his help. We don't know exactly what it was, but there are some clues in the book of Genesis.

"Joseph named his older son Manasseh, for he said, 'God had made me forget all of my troubles… (Genesis 41:51)'" I remember a few years back when I noticed this sentence for the first time. I had read it who knows how many times, but this one time was different. I thought to myself, "Why would someone name their firstborn son, 'God has caused me to forget?'" I know how much thought went into my kids' names. Whatever God did, Joseph wanted to be reminded of it every time he called his son's name.

The first time I looked at this passage I thought, "Can we really forget?" As in, does God wipe the memory of our pain from our minds like some sort of holy amnesia? I think the answer is no. I believe that Joseph remembered every single thing that his brothers did to him, down to the looks on their faces as they tossed him into the cistern to die. So why would he name his son, "God has caused me to forget?" I don't believe God wiped Joseph's mind, but he instead took the pain that was attached to those memories. The pain of betrayal had no power over Joseph anymore.

If Joseph, who dealt with pain unimaginable, can forgive and forget, then so can we. I'll try to explain what I think that process looks like with a scrapbooking analogy. Yes, you heard me right, a scrapbooking analogy. (Side note: Aimee used to love scrapbooking, so I have intimate knowledge of the mind of a scrapbooker.) You might be screaming with delight, "Finally, an author that truly gets me!" Or maybe not. Whatever your level of scrapbooking obsession I think you'll understand what I'm trying to communicate.

Imagine every painful memory you've ever had is a picture, and each one of those pictures is in a scrapbook that you keep hidden and safe in the arts and crafts room of your mind. You protect this scrapbook with everything in you because its contents keep you safe.

You may be wondering, "How do old pictures keep me safe?"

Well, these old pictures help you to recognize potential pain before it happens, which gives you the upper hand in avoiding it. They are your early warning system. You say, "If I forget the pain of my past, then I am more susceptible to future pain." This perfectly logical statement is the main reason why you protect your scrapbook pictures like a well-trained pit bull. But, as you'll remember from the last section, if you remove the possibility of pain from your life, you will remove the possibility of love. If you start something without love, you'll just make a lot of noise, and not a beautiful sounding noise (see 1st Corinthians 13:1). I don't want that for you.

If you're asking yourself how Joseph was able to tear up the pain pictures in his scrapbook. I'll let you know, it's not a walk in the park. It will feel like you are surrendering the only defenses you have left. It will stir up insecurities and fears that have been dormant in you for years. But honestly, you should have known loving your "enemies" was going to be a dangerous proposition.

Here is the process I think Joseph went through. Every one of us has a God-given time machine that we can use to travel to the future or the past. (Hint: it's your mind.) Joseph had to use his to travel back to the moment when one of his pain pictures was taken, the day his brothers betrayed him. He had to enter that moment again, a moment supercharged with emotion. All of the emotion of that moment, plus the secondary emotions that had built up over the years, joined forces in an attempt to take over his mind.

In the midst of all the pain, Joseph had to find a way to see the situation differently. He had to switch the position of his camera from his point of view to another. It's nearly impossible to forgive and forget without a change of perspective. At some point in his journey, Joseph decided to change his perspective to God's perspective. He proves it when he says to his brothers, "I am Joseph, your brother, whom you sold into slavery in Egypt. But don't be upset, and don't be angry with yourselves for selling me to this place. It was God who sent me here ahead of you to preserve your lives (Genesis 45:4-5)."

Joseph, because he allowed himself to see his pain through God's eyes, was transformed from revenge seeker to savior. He allowed the Holy Spirit to renew his mind in regards to his pain, and one by one he tore up the scrapbook pictures connected to that pain. As he destroyed each picture, the pain attached to those moments had less and less power over his decision making. Joseph was able to love and save his brothers instead of making them pay for what they had done.

We never know what effect our forgiveness can have on others. Sometimes we forgive just because it's the "right" thing to do (and it is), but it is more than that. If Joseph wouldn't have forgiven his brothers and carried out his revenge, then the twelve tribes of Israel would have never existed. Joseph could have snuffed out the nation of Israel before it even took its first breathe.

I'm sure, in that moment, Joseph had no idea how important his forgiveness would be to the future of mankind. He had no idea the savior of the world would come out of the nation he was preserving in the form of the brothers who had betrayed him. That same reality holds true for each of us. We have no idea what negative consequences our lack of forgiveness can create in the world.

To think of our own unforgiveness through the lens of Joseph's story is frightening, but it should also be challenging. Like Joseph, we have to begin to see our pain through the eyes of God, to gain His holy perspective. Once we allow that process to begin by surrendering our pain to him, we can begin to tear up the pictures that dominate our scrapbook. The pain won't have to dictate our decision making anymore, and we can be free to love. When we are free to love, we can replace those scattered pictures of pain with pictures of joy, trust, and forgiveness. Sounds like the beginning of a beautiful scrapbook.

Love is the foundation of it all. If we can't bring ourselves to the place of sacrificial love, then the whole idea of starting anything becomes a hollow and fruitless exercise. But if we fearlessly embrace the pain that comes with love – and forgive to the point where we can become vulnerable again – then anything is possible. People don't know what to do with love like that. There isn't a neat and tidy place in their brain for it, and so it bypasses the structures of their mind and begins to mess with their heart.

That type of love is available to you and me, and now is the time for us to get over ourselves and tap into that love. To try in every moment to do the most loving thing we can for the people we come into contact with everyday. To love until it hurts. To give our lives so that others might know love. To put others first and cut all of the strings attached to our "acts of service." To take ourselves out of the equation and allow someone else to occupy the center of the universe.

You can start something without love, but whatever it is it will end. For eternity to take hold of any earthly pursuit, that pursuit must have love as its motivation. Love was here at the beginning, and He will be here at the end. If you only remember one thing from this book, remember this: just love. If you are ever in a situation where you're not sure what the right thing to do is, just love. Don't think, just love.

PART 4

Where Do We Go From Here

10

What Do I Do Now?

Good question. I'm a practical person, so I am always trying to figure out how to apply revelation to my actual life. Revelation is worth less when it's stuck inside our minds. Hopefully by now, something inside of you has stirred. There are ripples forming on the surface of the still waters of your passion. Maybe you can't figure out what this new feeling is yet, but you're at least willing to test it to see if it's real.

I think a huge part of the "what now" or post-revelation stage of growth comes down to the willingness to test yourself. Being willing to take a chance on a feeling, to go with your gut. In my life, I've found it's the only way to get myself off the couch. I have to take a leap of faith because there will never be a sure thing, no matter how much I want there to be. I have to "gamble" on God coming through and being who He says He is.

This is the part of the book where we start to send electrical signals from our brains to our hands and feet and not just allow those signals to complete an endless loop in our mind. This is where we start to test ourselves a little, to see if this stuff really works. Don't worry; I'm convinced you can do this. We've known each other for ten chapters now, and I'm a very good judge of character.

In our last chapter together, we'll try to clarify some things that might have been lost in translation. We'll create a plan of attack, and then we'll do just that – attack.

WHAT I'M NOT SAYING

Before we get too far into this chapter, I want to make sure we're on the same page. (You see what I did there, that was a book pun.) I've tried my best to communicate clearly throughout this book, but in my experience it is always better to double check. So what follows is a list of things that I didn't say in this book. Just in case you made it to chapter ten thinking that I said, "Only astronauts go to heaven," I didn't say that.

I'll be using bullet points because I love bullet points. Bullet points just cut through all the noise, and get straight to the point (pun intended). So, to the little black dots we go!

- I didn't say that starting something looks like selling all of your stuff and moving to the other side of the world. It could look like that, but it won't look like that for everyone. You could become a doctor, run for city council, ride your bike seven hundred miles through California to raise money for a good cause, document injustice through the lens of a camera, publicly sing a song you wrote, or be the best mom ever.

- I didn't say that becoming a "missionary" is the highest calling. I don't believe in a hierarchy of callings. Therefore, I don't believe in one calling being higher than another. My desire is that each of us would pursue our own calling without fear, whatever that calling may be.

- I didn't say our sin doesn't matter. If you are currently stuck in a habitual pattern of sin, you need to take the steps necessary to break that pattern in your life. Talk to someone. Get help. Be transparent and allow the Holy Spirit to free you from it.

- I didn't say that starting something somehow makes you a better or more valuable person. I want to make sure you know that the reason to start something is to reveal your value to the world (and yourself), and in the process make an eternal impact on the lives of others. It's not to obtain your value by accomplishing things and thereby securing your eternity.

- I didn't say the pain you have experienced isn't valid or important. Your pain is real and your feelings about it are valid, but your pain (regardless of its origins or severity) should never stop you from freely loving others. In fact, my prayer is that your pain would fuel your love, not quench it.

- I certainly didn't say that any of this would be easy. I don't want you to get the idea that I have this all figured out, and you should just be able to figure it out too. No, I struggle with this stuff every day, but that doesn't make it any less true. I write about these things because I believe them. And we should fight for what we believe in, even if that fight is painful.

I'm sure I could write an entire book on things I didn't say, but I think this list is sufficient. My hope is that as you were reading that list you were thinking, "I didn't think he said any of these things!" If it makes you feel any better, I trust your comprehension and interpretation skills far more than my written communication skills. It's not you, it's me.

CREATE A FEAR BUCKET LIST

OK, we both know what a bucket list is, right? I assume we do, but my Grandma used to say assuming makes an a** out of you and me, so let's make sure just in case. A bucket list is a list of things you want to do before you die. The list is usually comprised of things like traveling to New Zealand, climbing Mount Kilimanjaro, sky diving, bungee jumping, seeing the Northern Lights, etc. The goal is to check everything off of the list before you kick the bucket (i.e. die). Kind of morbid.

I love the idea in principle. I have a sports version of the bucket list. (I am an unapologetic sports nerd if you haven't picked that up yet.) It's a list of sports teams, stadiums, and experiences that I want to witness before I go to heaven, such as watch the Sydney Swans play at the MCG (Melbourne Cricket Ground), watch the All Blacks do the "Haka" at Eden Park, and watch Liverpool beat Manchester United at Anfield (no apologies to my friends that are United fans).

A normal bucket list, just like my sports bucket list, isn't necessarily a bunch of things you are trying to avoid in life. It's usually a list of dreams you haven't made time for, but when you realize that your remaining time on earth is limited, you put forth the effort to accomplish them.

A fear bucket list is a little different. Instead of a list of dreams, it's closer to a list of nightmares. (As I was typing that sentence it seemed too intense, but when I read it again I was like, "Yep, that's it.") It's a list of things you have spent your life avoiding, a list of things that have dictated the choices you've made and influenced the dreams you were willing to pursue. But instead of choosing to take detours around the things on this list, you are choosing to drive straight at each chill-inducing nightmare.

To illustrate, let me tell you an embarrassing story from my childhood. When I was young, one of our neighbors would use the land around our house to graze his cattle. It wasn't a large herd, maybe only thirty head, but to me it seemed like hundreds. There weren't any bulls in the herd, just cows, but among the cows there were always a few that, from my little kid perspective, acted like bulls.

I'm just going to be honest (try not to laugh); I was scared half to death by those cows. I was so afraid that for much of my childhood I had nightmares involving cows. I can't count how many times I stumbled into my parents' room after I had woken up from a dream where I was being chased by bloodthirsty bovines. My fear of cows got so bad that I started making decisions on where I would play based on whether or not I had people with me. I wasn't brave enough to face my tormentors on my own.

It all changed one night as I was having another one of my cow nightmares. I remember running from the herd towards my house, sprinting up the sand pit hill and taking a shortcut through the barbed-wire fence. As I approached my front door, this strange thought shot through my dreamscape. "This isn't real." In that moment, for the first time in years, I realized I had the power to change my circumstances. So I did.

In a flash, I spun around and started walking directly at the leader of the herd, closer and closer until I was face to face with my stunned enemy. My apologies to animal rights activists for this next part, but I started beating the living manure out of any cow that was in swinging distance of me. One by one they fell until none remained. I never had another bad dream about cows. I didn't know it at the time, but I had officially checked the first box on my fear bucket list.

I'm sure your list will include more rational fears than my own, but that doesn't change the fact that you have the power over your list of fears and not the other way around. The sooner you stop running from whatever herd is chasing you, the sooner you will realize the power you possess.

Paul wrote to Timothy, "For God has not given us a spirit of fear or timidity, but of power, love, and self discipline (2 Timothy 1:17)." He has given you the power to overcome your list of fears. He hasn't made you timid; He has made you an intimidator. It's time to tap into that power and turn and face your own herd of fears. It's time to start swinging haymakers until you've connected with the jaw of every antagonist standing in your path. (Remember, I'm talking about dream punches, not real ones. Don't punch anyone in real life, please.) If my eight year old self can do it, so can you.

So, step one, start compiling a Fear Bucket List. Start writing down all the things that petrify you, the things that make you want to hide in a corner when you think about them, the things that make you change your plans in order to avoid them. Your list could include giving a speech in public, sitting in an airplane as it cruises at 35,000 feet, looking down from the top floor of the Empire State Building, or falling in love again. It doesn't really matter what it is, if it's standing in your way, put it on the list.

I'll assume you've already started sweating as you begin to process the task in front of you, but don't get ahead of yourself. Just take a second, grab a pen and paper and start writing. Don't think about what it's going to take to check some of these fears off of your list, just focus on getting them out of your brain and onto the page. When you feel you have made sufficient progress on your list, you have my permission to move onto the next section. No cheating.

PRESS YOUR ADVENTURE BUTTON

Thanks for taking care of that fear bucket list I asked for. We need to cover one more thing before we start to tackle that list. It has to do with how we see our circumstances, and it can have a direct effect on how enjoyable this fear squashing ride turns out to be.

I'm sure you're asking, "What in the world is an adventure button, and if I have one, how can I get it removed?" Let me explain. When I was an intern director a few years back, part of my job was preparing our intern mission teams for overseas travel. We would get together once a week to pray and learn. There would be discussions on topics like culture shock, acclimatizing, language, customs, etc. Most of the students were overcoming some type of fear by signing up to go on the trip. But they each felt like God was calling them, so they made the decision to go anyway.

You see, whenever we embark on a fear conquering journey our natural inclination is to focus on ourselves. The purpose for making the journey in the first place is usually a love for God and people, but the discomfort that comes when we face our fears can cause us to become self-centered, whiny, and irritable. Kind of like when we skip lunch.

In order to combat this phenomenon, one of the topics I would teach on was "pressing your adventure button." I didn't put too much thought into the exact phrasing. It just basically popped into my head while I was teaching, and I decided to go with it.

What I meant by adventure button was the spot in our mind that controls how we see our circumstances. Like a perspective controlling device. When our adventure button is off, we think about our own comfort. When our adventure button is on, we think about the comfort of others. When our adventure button is off, we are more focused on the destination. When our adventure button is on, we are more focused on the journey. When our adventure button is off, we think more about safety and security. When our adventure button is on, we think more about...well, adventure!

Earlier in the book we talked about seeing obstacles as opportunities. That is exactly why the adventure button was made. When pressed, it changes how we perceive our world.

Let's say you are traveling to India for the first time. As your flight is about to taxi out onto runway "one niner niner," you hear a message from the captain. "Uh, folks, this is your captain speaking. We have a bit of a technical problem, and we're looking at about a 45 minute delay. Thank you for your patience." (Side note: Don't you just love when people thank you for your patience before you give it to them? I guess it sounds better than thanking you for your self-centered frustration.) You immediately realize you are going to miss your connecting flight in London.

If your adventure button is switched off: You focus on your personal inconvenience, the sudden lack of adequate ventilation, and the blatant armrest hogging of the passenger next to you as you translate the words "technical problem" into "midair engine failure" in your mind. If your adventure button is switched on: You realize what a privilege it is to even be able to fly on an airplane in the first place, that the passenger sitting next to you is a unique person with a unique story (I'm not saying you should have a deep conversation with every person you sit next to on an airplane, but you know what I'm saying.), and that the extra few hours in London might afford you the opportunity to see the city.

Or, imagine you travel to a developing country. Adventure button off: The fact that stores close early on Sundays – or don't open at all – frustrates you. The scheduled power outages and inconsistency of your Wi-Fi signal are about to send you over the edge. You spend most days complaining, and wishing that it was more like _____ (fill in the blank with whatever country you're from). Adventure button on: You love the fact that everything slows down on Sundays, and you use the power and Wi-Fi outages to spend more time talking with friends, and playing your acoustic guitar (the only thing in your life that still functions without a Wi-Fi signal and a power cord).

When you choose to step out of your comfort zone, you are bound to encounter situations that you weren't prepared for, situations that push you to your limits. A little pinch of perspective can make the difference between a life of hope and anticipation or a life of dread and frustration.

If you truly want to start something, then my advice is to press your adventure button. Once you say yes to God and start tackling some of your fears, the ride only gets crazier and crazier. Your instinct will be to say, "Safety first!" and pull the ripcord on your parachute. But instead, spread your arms out wide and lean into that free fall. Who knows, you might actually enjoy it.

TRY STUFF (CLIFF JUMPING)

A few years ago I was watching a soccer game between the Seattle Sounders (Go Sounders!) and some other MLS team that I like less than the Sounders. Seattle had just signed a new player, Clint Dempsey, and the announcers were discussing what made him so good. They talked about his technique, his elusiveness, and his eye for goal. Then one of the commentators shared a story of a conversation he had with someone who had played with Dempsey. It went something like this.

Color Commentator: "What makes Clint so special?"

Random Dempsey teammate: "He isn't afraid to try [stuff]."

You can probably figure out why the word "stuff" is in brackets. That wasn't exactly what he said, but it's close enough for our purposes.

The announcer was highlighting that the major difference between Dempsey and his peers wasn't necessarily his training, skills, or physical attributes. It was his mentality. He wouldn't let the fear of failure keep him from trying a trick or taking an unthinkable shot, which opened the door to special moments on the field.

We always assume that it takes special people to create special moments. This is true in the sense that we are all special. But what I mean is the people with qualities no one else possesses. The super people. You really don't have to be super to create special moments. In fact, special moments are created by courageous people. People who are willing to overcome their fears and take a leap of faith. People who aren't necessarily fearless but who have made a choice to not allow fear to dictate their future. I call these people cliff jumpers.

What does it take to transform from a fearful, excuse making cliff-clinger to a courageous cliff jumper? It starts with your faith. What you believe dictates your ability to transform.

Let me give you an example. Imagine that your entire life you have believed a lie. The lie is simple but effective. "I'm stupid." You've believed it for so long that it has become truth to you. Because of this, a series of "intelligence cliffs" are created within your mind. These cliffs are built on a lie and fortified by fear. An "intelligence cliff" could sound like, "I can't do that, I'm too stupid." Your belief in this lie dictates that, instead of jumping into the terrible blackness below, you retreat from the edge of the cliff, all the while reinforcing the foundations of the lie.

The only way to change the status quo in your mind is to allow a seed of belief, contrary to the lie, to begin to germinate. You have to make room in your mind for a maybe. "Maybe I'm not stupid." We discussed this in the chapter on identity. You and I have to believe somewhere inside of us that maybe we were made for this. Only then can we approach the edge of the cliffs in our minds, stare into the darkness below, and jump.

The scariest part about the leap is that you can never know for sure until you jump. You will never know if you are intelligent while still standing on the cliff. Your "maybe" will remain just that, a "maybe." If you want to turn your "maybe" into a "yes," you have to jump. If you want to know if you're smart enough to do something, anything, then you have to jump to find out.

Luckily, there is an added bonus to cliff jumping. It's not the cool suits you get to wear or the adrenaline rush that accompanies it. It's the fact that the scariest and most difficult jump you will ever make is your first. The second jump is easier than the first, the third easier than the second, the fourth easier than the third, and so on. Each time you courageously jump into the unknown, you fall head first into knowing. With each leap you learn something more about yourself. As the lies shrink, the truth about yourself grows until "I'm stupid" is replaced by "I'm smart."

Transforming the words "I'm stupid" into "I'm smart," might not seem significant, but it could be the difference between staying at home or embarking on the adventure of a lifetime. Making that transformation isn't just about telling yourself a thousand times that you're smart until you believe it, it's about making choices and taking risks that contradict the lies you've believed about yourself. It's about trying stuff that only smart people would try.

Remember that list of fears I told you to work on earlier? At the center of each one of those fears is a lie you've believed about yourself. Imagine the height of the cliff that those fear-inducing lies have created. You'll never know if any of those fears are real until you test them. So let your seed-sized faith push you to the edge of that cliff. Take a deep breath, and...

I'll let you take it from here.

Mathu Ardis Thomason

Instagram: @mathuardis

Twitter: @mathuthomason

Contact: mathuthomason@gmail.com

Made in the USA
Lexington, KY
28 April 2017